What people are saying

I found this book to be very insightful and u[...]
for a "higher path" through life.

As a college student I found this book very helpful. These 15 people have lived what they profess! Many others profess something but have never lived it.

If this "wisdom for the heart and soul" is like future issues in this series, I will buy them all!

What a crafty piece of work! These guys have assembled a work that is potentially life changing for anyone who wishes to become better informed and more aware of how to improve his or her life.

I believe every young adult should read this book. It can serve as a ready reference throughout life.

A very informative addition to the body of literature devoted to self-improvement...quite diverse, yet easy to assimilate.

This book has a great deal of potential. My husband and I gained a lot of insight from it—-and have recommended it to many of our friends.

We sincerely hope this book gets wide circulation. It has tremendous potential for informing and guiding those who could use a "nudge" in the right direction.

This was delightful reading. I learned about the lives of important people and felt uplifted by how they lived and the legacy they left.

As Pastoral counselors we found this book to be inspiring. It can serve as a remark-ably helpful guide for persons seeking to become more informed, aware, and further along toward self-understanding and an improved life.

As a medical doctor, I have devoted my life to improving physical health. This book will certainly help readers improve their spiritual and emotional health.

A career in the real estate industry has taught me a great deal about people. This book taught me a great deal about fifteen very important people—and what they said/did that might help me live a better life.

I only wish I had this book forty years ago as I was struggling with "How to Get a Life". My experiences would have been greatly enhanced with this primer in hand.

In my thirty years as a minister with the Disciples of Christ I have read many inform-ative and uplifting books—-this one fits both categories perfectly.

How to
Get a Life

How to Get a Life

Empowering Wisdom for the Heart and Soul

According to:

Mother Teresa
Jesus
Martin Luther King, Jr.
Joseph Campbell
Bill Wilson
Gerda Weissmann Klein
Albert Schweitzer
Oprah Winfrey

Buddha
Leo Buscaglia
Jane Goodall
Dalai Lama
Muhammad
Confucius
Richard of St. Victor

Edited by
Lawrence Baines, Ph.D.
Daniel McBrayer, Ph.D.

HUMANICS

How to Get a Life
A Humanics Trade Group Publication
© 2003 by Brumby Holdings, Inc.
First Edition

Humanics Trade Group Publications is an imprint of and published by Humanics Publishing Group, a division of Brumby Holdings, Inc. Its trademark, consisting of the words "Humanics Trade Group" and the portrayal of a pegasus, is registered in the U.S. Patent and Trademark Office and in other countries.

Brumby Holdings, Inc.
1197 Peachtree St.
Suite 533B
Atlanta, GA 30361
USA

Printed in the United States of America and the United Kingdom

ISBN (Paperback) 0-89334-389-7
ISBN (Hardcover) 0-89334-390-0

Library of Congress Control Number:2003108315

TABLE OF CONTENTS

Written By

INTRODUCTION

How do you get a life? Most people trudge through life without ever asking themselves the question. "The unexamined life," according to Socrates, "is not worth living." Most of us get up in the morning, eat breakfast, put in long hours at work, come home and watch television, fall asleep, then wake up the next morning and repeat the process for the next 15,000 or so days until retirement. Many of us dislike our jobs (or other aspects of life), but endure them to keep bread on the table or to insure that our children have enough money for college. There may be a better path through life!

For those who have the courage and drive to ponder the possibilities of getting a life, a starting point might be where you find yourself today in terms of work, spirituality, love, family, relationships, achievements, money, community, health, and hobbies. Most of us measure the quality of our lives by comparing our dreams against what we have accomplished in each of these areas.

When the distance from where you happen to find yourself at the moment is a thousand miles from your dreams, you may feel distressed and disappointed. However, as is evident from the lives of the eminent men and women in this book, it is never too late to get a life. As you read this, you might be at a crossroads without a clue of which direction to take next. All of us have been there.

From Lawrence: I was in my late-twenties and had been teaching English and coaching team sports at a secondary school for eight years. Although I found my role as teacher and coach to be challenging and satisfying, I was growing restless. "What am I doing here? What should I do with my life? Is this all there is to life? What do I want to accomplish before I die?"

One day while eating lunch in the school cafeteria, I jotted down some possible careers on a sheet of paper—surfing instructor in Hawaii, concert pianist, professor, artist, more years as a high school teacher and coach. I weighed each career with utter seriousness and devised a point system to evaluate the alternatives. Although surfing instructor in Hawaii garnered the most points, I found it difficult to ascertain precisely why I might choose surfing over another path. Was there something more to life than great weather and enjoying the ride in the middle of a 15-foot wave? I needed some guidance, but didn't know where to turn.

That evening, I went to the bookstore and purchased a copy of Plato's *The Republic*, which I had somehow missed in college. I had heard that *The Republic* was a "foundational book," instructive about the art of living. Although I was motivated to read *The Republic* and dutifully highlighted eloquent passages in bright yellow, it took me a month of late-nights and weekends to slog through it all. After I finished, I knew a little more about ethics, the virtues of living a rational life, and Socrates' ideas for good government. But I was no closer to making a decision about my life than when I initially picked up the book. To be honest, I still didn't care a great deal about Plato; what I wanted was to learn something that would be useful in my own life. Surf instructor or concert pianist? I quit my job at the school and enrolled in graduate school.

*From Dan:*I was the middle of nine children and grew up on a farm in a rural community in South Dakota. I loved farm life, but knew that if I stayed on the farm, I would be welded to that parcel of land for the rest of my days. Before I agreed to don the overalls for good, I wanted to discover what the world was like outside of South Dakota. Will Rogers said that there are two ways to raise your intelligence: (a) Hang out with folks smarter than you, (b) Read, read, read. Given that there were so few opportunities to interact with people outside my immediate family in the outback where we lived, I decided that I needed to start cracking some books. Once I began reading I discovered a "whole new world" beyond the bubble of my secure and sheltered existence. Reading—and later, travel—changed me forever. I began to figure out how to get a life in mid-adulthood and I am still working on it. Along the way, I have discovered that part of getting a life for me involves teaching, forging relationships with students, and making people smile. However, I continue to believe that work and relationships are only two of the ingredients for "getting a life." What is in my heart, soul, and mind dictate what I do in work, relationships, and all other aspects of life.

How to Get a Life: Empowering Wisdom for the Heart and Soul is the first volume in a series of books that are designed to help guide you toward a more fulfilling life. *How to Get a Life* is the resource that neither of us had when we reached that point in life when we were ready to make a change, but had no idea how to bring it about. An "executive summary" of the lives of fifteen eminent people and a practical "self-help" book, *How to Get a Life* describes how the beliefs and habits of some courageous men and women helped elevate them beyond mediocrity. These are the lessons of lifetimes, brimming with hope for a better tomorrow, and a portentous sense of destiny. Perhaps if we had had this resource, we might have struggled less and enjoyed more!

Because the humanities and the arts are cumulative, the list of "essential books" grows daily. The philosophy of the Dalai Lama does not supplant the work of Mother Teresa, which in turn, does not negate the work of Martin Luther King, Jr. or Albert Schweitzer. Each offers a unique vision of the human condition that has managed to endure over time. Rare is the individual today who has the time to read and contemplate the complete works of any one writer, let alone the hundreds of thousands of new books published annually. *How to Get a Life* can help you fill in the gaps by giving you an overview of the life and times of individuals who have changed forever how we think about the heart and soul.

The spiritual leaders and humanitarians in *How to Get a Life* share a passion for living and a personal ethic for success. This is not to say that they are perfect, squeaky-clean human beings, but the focus is upon how these powerful leaders managed their lives and changed the world. We purposefully chose an eclectic group of men and women, from the well-known to the relatively obscure, from the secular to the divine.

When you enter old age, you have the advantage of having witnessed firsthand how the lives of your friends turned out. The passing of time provides a unique vantage point from which to view the trajectory of a life—how what you believe and what you do in a day affects your outlook, pocketbook, the lines in your face, and the shape of your soul. By reading about the lives of men and women who have lived over the past two thousand years or so, we hope to provide you with a similar kind of "broadening" experience.

How to Get a Life offers a rich repository of advice when the dragon crosses your path, when you feel directionless, or when you are feeling a little too comfortable with the world. It does not matter if you decide to follow a particular individual's advice for living, if you decide to synthesize a variety of perspectives, or if you reject them all. What matters is deciding upon the life you want, then working towards its realization. *How To Get A Life: Empowering Wisdom for the Heart and Soul* offers the stories of fifteen men and women who obtained their dreams, then lived in them.

Each chapter in *How to Get a Life* stands alone. You may wish to begin on page one and read the chapters in order, or if you are predisposed to learn about a specific individual, you may begin at that chapter and skip around randomly. We believe that you will want to keep this book in your personal collection because you can return to it throughout your life to review the wisdom of some powerful individuals. To glean the most from the book, we suggest reading a chapter at a time, reflecting on it, and perhaps jot down some notes.

The first step in getting a life is deciding you want one. As you begin your journey, it may be useful to remember some lines from Joseph Campbell (who is included in this volume).

> You enter the forest at the darkest point where there is no path. Where there is a way or path it is somebody else's path. You are not on your own path. If you follow someone else's way, you are not going to realize your potential (Campbell and Osbon, 1991, 22).

References and Resources

Campbell, J. & Osbon D. ed. 1991. *A Joseph Campbell Companion*. New York: HarperCollins.

How to
Get a Life

A/P World Wide Photos

MOTHER TERESA
(1910-1997)

By Jennie M. Smith

By the time she died in 1997, Mother Teresa had captivated the hearts of millions throughout the world with her work among the poor and destitute. Born Agnes Gonxha Bojaxhiu to a devout Catholic family in Albania, she sensed very early in her life that God was calling her to serve Him by caring for others. At age eighteen, she became a nun and went to Calcutta. Eventually, she left her work at the convent to serve the poor in the surrounding slums, and in 1950 she founded the Society of the Missionaries of Charity. By 1952, she and her Sisters were establishing centers aimed at caring for the dying, abandoned and orphaned children, and lepers. Their work gradually expanded to include many other types of ministry and spread across the globe. Among the many honors Mother Teresa received was the 1979 Noble Peace Prize. In Something Beautiful for God, Malcolm Muggeridge (1971) offers the description of Mother Teresa: "She, a nun, rather slightly built, with a few rupees in her pocket; not particularly clever, or particularly gifted in the arts of persuasion. Just with this Christian love shining about her; in her heart and on her lips" (22).

> There's a light in this world, a healing spirit more powerful than any darkness we may encounter. We sometimes lose sight of this force when there is suffering, too much pain. Then suddenly, the spirit will emerge through the lives of ordinary people who hear a call, and answer in extraordinary ways (opening narration for the 1987 television film, *Mother Teresa*).

One of the things I remember most about the hours I spent in the Missionaries of Charity AIDS hospice in Port-au-Prince, Haiti, is the light— the sunlight coming in through the large open windows and reflecting off the recently scrubbed concrete floors; the light in the eyes of the sari-clothed Sisters; the bright, clean suds of shampoo the Sisters gently massaged into the scalps of the residents. Located in the midst of one of Port-au-Prince's many sprawling, overcrowded neighborhoods, this place was a haven not just for the residents but also for the volunteers. It reminded us that there is, indeed, light left in this world and that the continued existence of that light depends not on the heavens, nor on chance, but on our willingness to be its hosts.

Turning Points

Agnes Gonxha Bojaxhiu began her life in 1910 in Skopje, Albania. She was the daughter of Kolë and Drana Bojaxhiu. When Agnes was only nine years old, her father unexpectedly died, leaving Drana to care for Agnes and Agnes' sister and brother. Drana resolved to bring up the children under the wing of the Catholic Church. Daily she led them in prayers and took them to mass. Despite the difficulties Drana faced as a single parent trying to raise three children on a modest budget, she also cared for others in Skopje who were less fortunate than her own struggling family. Agnes enjoyed worshipping, praying, singing and serving the poor alongside her mother.

Agnes eventually felt called to become a nun, and in 1928 journeyed to Dublin, Ireland, to join the Loreto Sisters. She would never again see her mother and sister. It was in Dublin that she changed her name to Teresa, in memory of Little Teresa of Lisieux, a nineteenth century saint who praised the beauty and value of serving God in "little ways." Soon she was sent from Dublin to Bengal, where she joined the faculty of the Loreto Sisters' St. Mary's School for Girls in Calcutta. Teresa was happy and comfortable at the school. She enjoyed teaching courses in geography and later, serving as the school's principal. As time went by, however, she found herself increasingly drawn outside the walls of the peaceful convent and into the bustling streets of the surrounding slums, which she found to be teeming with poverty and human suffering. Whenever she could, Teresa walked those streets and ministered to the women, men and children she found there, sometimes bringing them food, medicines, or other supplies from the convent.

On September 10, 1946, after years of struggling internally to reconcile her calling with the human suffering she saw about her, Teresa received a revelation from God that would change the course of her life. In that revelation, she later reported, God told her that she must leave the convent and devote herself to serving the poorest of the poor. Two more years passed before she finally received permission from Rome to follow this command. Soon thereafter, a number of Teresa's former pupils joined her in the slums of Calcutta, and in 1950, the Vatican approved the establishment of the Society of the Missionaries of Charity. Beginning with twelve Sisters and virtually no financial or material resources, Teresa (now Mother Teresa) established Nirmal Hriday, the first Home for the Destitute and Dying. Before long, foundations for lepers and for abandoned and orphaned children emerged. By 1965, Mother Teresa and her sisters were establishing missions overseas.

Even as she became physically frail, Mother Teresa continued to plunge herself into some of the world's most difficult regions—those devastated by war (West Beruit, 1982), AIDS (Greenwich Village, 1985), famine (Ethiopia, 1985), and toxic pollution (Chernobyl, 1986). By the time she died in 1997, she and her followers had built a world-wide network of over 5,000 Sisters and thousands more Brothers, lay missionaries and volunteers. They were working in 120 countries throughout the globe, and were running 569 missions aimed at serving the physical and spiritual needs of the dying, the homeless, orphaned and abandoned children, battered women, prostitutes, and those suffering from leprosy, AIDS, mental illness, physical deformity, tuberculosis, drug addiction, and alcoholism. In Mother Teresa's eyes, the growth of her humanitarian efforts was a credit neither to herself nor her followers, but to God. She was, she insisted, "a pencil in God's hand." Since Mother Teresa's death, Sister Nirmala, an Indian Hindu who converted to Christianity, has served as the Missionaries' Superior General. Mother Teresa remains the Society's symbolic and spiritual head.

Principles to Live By

What does Mother Teresa have to teach us—you and me, Christian and non-Christian, intellectual and professional, Easterner and Westerner, young and old—about How to Get a Life? My exploration of that question is grounded in a number of phrases Mother Teresa repeated hundreds of times throughout her life:

> Make us worthy, Lord, to serve our fellow men throughout the world who live and die in poverty and hunger. Give them, through our hands, this day their daily bread, and by our understanding love, give peace and joy.

This was one of Mother Teresa's several daily prayers, and highlights a number of the main principles that guided her life. The first of those principles is humility. Too often, when we are engaged in "helping others," we operate with the assumption that we are doing "others" a favor and not the other way around. In her prayer, Mother Teresa makes it clear that serving others is a grace we receive, not a favor we bestow. It is something for which we should be thankful, not something for which we should expect thanks. Mother Teresa emphasizes that we should strive to be worthy of service. Helping others does not translate into perfect understanding of another's needs. Genuine insight can be a painstakingly slow process, and requires guidance and sensitivity.

Many of the most pressing needs in the world today are spiritual rather than material. The world needs "understanding love" at least as much as it needs bread. To the surprise of many who visited Mother Teresa in the squalor of Calcutta, she insisted that "The biggest disease today is not leprosy or tuberculosis, but rather the feeling of being unwanted, uncared for and deserted by everybody. The greatest evil is the lack of love and charity, the terrible indifference towards one's neighbor" (Muggeridge, 1971, 74). Particularly in the "developed countries," she pointed out, "there is poverty of intimacy, a poverty of spirit, of loneliness, of lack of love" (Balado, 1996, 89). Suffering is not only to be found in slums, prisons or brothels, Mother Teresa liked to say. A poverty of spirit may well be located within your own neighborhood, and in many cases, within your own household. "We need to find God, and he cannot be found in noise and restlessness. God is the friend of silence …. The more we receive in silent prayer, the more we can give in our active life."

"Make us worthy, Lord …" is only one among the many daily prayers of the Missionaries of Charity. In fact, the Sisters devote several hours of every day to prayer. No matter how pressing the tasks before them, no matter if they are right in the middle of doing several tasks at once—when the time arrives for prayers, the Sisters drop everything and gather quietly to commune with God. More than sleep, more than food, the commitment to prayer, they say, gives them the strength they need to face—day after long day—the heart-wrenching, labor-intensive work they perform. "Prayer is not asking," Mother Teresa said, "Prayer is putting oneself in the hands of God, at his disposition, and listening to his voice in the depths of our heart" (Balado, 1996, 9). Through prayer, we put ourselves "completely under the influence of Jesus so that [we] may think his thoughts in'[our] mind[s], do his work with [our] hands" (Muggeridge, 1971, 67).

Even though Mother Teresa's prayers were unwaveringly Christian, and though she sought to lead others to Christ, she encouraged those of other faiths to pray in their own ways. "I've always said that we should help a Hindu become a better Hindu, a Muslim become a better Muslim, a Catholic become a better Catholic" (Vardey, 1995, 33). To grow spiritually, you must spend time in quiet communion with the Divine. "Each individual person has been created to love and to be loved—Hindu, Muslim, Jew, Christian—doesn't matter race, doesn't matter religion. Every single man, woman, child is the child of God, created in the image of God."

Despite recent trends toward an embrace of multiculturalism in America, racism and ethnocentrism are still widespread, in America and throughout the world. What will it take to finally rid the world of these plagues? More lawsuits? More diplomacy? More free market trade? Or something much more radical—and simple—than any of the solutions commonly posited by our leaders? Perhaps our only hope lies in learning to believe as seriously as Mother Teresa did that most basic and most radical of Christian tenets: that we are all—each and every one of us—God's children. "To show great love for God and our neighbor we need not do great things. It is how much love we put into the doing that makes our offering something beautiful for God."

During the first few years I spent in Haiti, I worked alongside several other North Americans in a rural community development program. All but one of our group played an active role in the administration of the program. Among our responsibilities were teaching lessons on topics like preventing neonatal tetanus; diarrhea and protein-deficiency; demonstrating sustainable tillage techniques; advocating the use of natural fertilizers; capping underground springs for potable water; encouraging residents to participate in local and national democratization; and trekking many miles over mountainous footpaths to attend thousands of community meetings. We worked long, hard hours and prided ourselves on our work's results. It was close to the end of my three-year term in this project that I learned a surprising fact. According to many of the locals, it was the one non-program-affiliated person—Carla—who most benefited the community. The spouse of an agriculturalist, Carla spent most of her days in and around her family's home, taking care of her three children and socializing with neighbors who stopped by for a visit, or to partake in a bit of milk, rice, or medicine.

"Carla always greeted us well," people said. She usually offered a smile, a cool drink of water, and often a treat or two. "She is gracious." "She really cares about us." They were telling us, as Mother Teresa does, that "It is not how much you do but how much love you put into the doing and sharing with others that is important" (Vardey, 1995, 93).

The examples of Mother Teresa and Carla challenge us to step away from our rush towards success, and reassess our work on an altogether different basis. Rather than monetary advantage, the questions become, Does it make others feel cared for? Does it tell them that they are loved? Does it acknowledge that they—that all of us—are children of the Divine?

Mother Teresa's commitment to doing small things with great love was the foundation on which the Missionaries of Charity and their ministries were built. Day by day, act by act, Mother Teresa showed that by bandaging the sores of a dying man, feeding a homeless orphan, comforting a mother who has lost her son to warfare, one person can change the world. "Begin in a small way," [Mother Teresa] directed those who worked with her. "Don't look for numbers" (Middleton, 2001, 51).

For many, Mother Teresa's prioritization of "great love" over "great acts" was her ministry's most unique—and most attractive—component. Each year thousands of people traveled from points across the globe simply to mop floors, empty urinals, massage sore limbs, feed empty bellies, and to work with Mother Teresa and the Sisters. Most left with their hearts transformed by their experience. One of Mother Teresa's helpers once wrote, "I was as overwhelmed with her simplicity and her determination ... She saw God's face in every human being. All were children of God to her ... I got peace" (*Las Vegas Review-Journal*, September 6, 1997).

There could be no better way to honor Mother Teresa than to embrace the opportunity to serve and to live a life true to our consciences, consistent with our understanding of Divine love, and most respectful of those we would serve.

When the Road is Smooth

It is no accident that Mother Teresa rarely traveled down smooth roads. Unlike most of us, she actively sought to locate her journey on some of the world's "rockiest" social, political and economic terrain—places of war, famine, disease and loneliness. Her advice to the traveler of the smooth road, then, would likely be to stop, look around, look inside, look to God and ask whether this is the road God has called him or her to travel. The answer is likely to be no.

When the Road Gets Rocky

When the road was most rocky, windy, and strewn with gullies, Mother Teresa found strength in her absolute certainty that she was living God's will. This certainty allowed her to cherish the work of mending oozing wounds and sitting long hours at the bedsides of the dying. During these rocky times, Mother Teresa always kept her "eye on the prize"—the prize being not some lofty heavenly reward, but rather the gift of being able to serve the poorest and most needy.

When You Encounter a Dragon in the Middle of the Road

Mother Teresa's advice for what to do when difficulties and confrontations come your way was to pray, and then to follow—small step by small step—the guidance received thereby. She would most likely recommend to us the following prayer of St. Francis of Assisi, which she recited daily.

Lord, make me a channel of Thy peace,
that where there is hatred, I may bring love;
that where there is wrong, I may bring the spirit of forgiveness;
that where there is discord, I may bring harmony;
that where there is error, I may bring truth;
that where there is doubt, I may bring faith;
that where there is despair, I may bring hope;
that where there are shadows, I may bring light;
that where there is sadness, I may bring joy.

9

Lord, grant that I may seek rather to comfort than to be comforted,
to understand than to be understood, to love than to be loved;

For it is by forgetting self that one finds;
it is by forgiving that one is forgiven;
it is by dying that one awakens to eternal life.

The Crux

According to Mother Teresa, the crux of her message was contained
in the text written on her personal business cards (Crimp, 2000).
The fruit of silence is prayer.
The fruit of prayer is faith.
The fruit of faith is love.
The fruit of love is service.
The fruit of service is peace.

In a Nutshell

"She is, so transparently, someone who eschews the values of our age
where success in life is measured by the number of trappings acquired and in
so doing she offers us hope that spirituality, not materialism, will triumph;
hope that there are higher standards we can aspire to; and hope that maybe
one day all the children in the world will be fed" (Sebba, 1998, xiii).

The Wisdom of Mother Teresa (quotations are from *In My Own Words*)

On Holiness
Holiness is not the luxury of a few. It is everyone's duty: yours and
mine.

On Prayer
Prayer is not asking. Prayer is putting oneself in the hands of God,
at his disposition, and listening to his voice in the depths of our
hearts.

On Serving the Poor

Today it is very fashionable to talk about the poor. Unfortunately, it is not fashionable to talk with them.

On Looking in the Mirror

The Poor call to us. We have to be aware of them in order to love them. We have to ask ourselves if we know the truth. Do we know the poor in our own homes?

On Money

Someone once told me that not even for a million dollars would they touch a leper. I responded: "Neither would I. If it were a case of money, I would not even do it for two million. On the other hand, I do it gladly for love of God."

On Poverty

I will never tire of repeating this: what the poor need the most is not pity but love. They need to feel respect for their human dignity, which is neither less nor different from the dignity of any other human being.

On Hunger

The world today is hungry not only for bread, but hungry for love; hungry to be wanted, to be loved.

On Love

Spread love everywhere you go: first of all in your own house. Give love to your children, to your wife or husband, to a next door neighbor .... Let no one come to you without leaving better or happier. Be the living expression of God's kindness; kindness in your face, kindness in your eyes, kindness in your smile and kindness in your warm greeting.

On God

Give yourself fully to God. He will use you to accomplish great things on the condition that you believe much more in his love than in your own weakness (as cited in Crimp 2000, 74).

Important Dates

1910	Born Agnes Gonxha Bojaxhiu in Skopje, Macedonia.
1928	Entered the Sisters of Loreto order in Ireland and began her novitiate in India.
1929-1948	Teacher and principal at St. Mary's High School in Calcutta.
1948	Received permission from the Catholic Church to live out side the school and serve "the poorest of the poor."
1950	Received approval for the Society of the Missionaries of Charity.
1952	Established the first Missionaries of Charity home (Nirmal Hriday) in Calcutta.
1965	Established the first home outside India, in Cocorote, Venezuela. She and the Sisters would eventually establish missions in over 120 nations around the world, including the United States and several European countries.
1979	Awarded the Nobel Peace Prize.
1997	Died in Calcutta, India.

References and Resources

Crimp, S. 2000. *Touched by a Saint: Personal Encounters with Mother Teresa*. Notre Dame: Sorin Books.

Gjergji, L. 1998. *Mother Teresa: To Live, to Love, to Witness—Her Spiritual Way*. Jordan Aumann, trans. Hyde Park: New City Press.

González, B. & Luis, J. 1996. *Mother Teresa: In My Own Words*. New York: Gramercy Books.

Le Joly, E. 1998(1977). *We Do it for Jesus: Mother Teresa and Her Missionaries of Charity (2nd edition)*. Delhi: Oxford University Press.

Middleton, H. 2001. *Mother Teresa: An Unauthorized Biography*. Chicago: Heinemann Library.

Mother Teresa & Cervantes, S. 1997. *Mother Teresa: In My Own Words: 1910 – 1997*. New York; Random House.

Muggeridge, M. 1971. *Something Beautiful for God*. New York: Harper and Row.

Rai, R. & Chawla, N. 1996. *Faith and Compassion: The Life and Works of Mother Teresa*. Shaftesbury, Dorset: Element.

Sebba, A. 1998. *Mother Teresa: Beyond the Image*. New York: Image Books (Doubleday).

Stanovsky, D. 1999. "Princess Diana, Mother Teresa, and the Value of Women's
    Work." *NWSA Journal* 11(2): 146-151.
Vardey, L. 1995. *Mother Teresa: A Simple Path*. New York: Ballantine Books.

For more information on Mother Teresa and for pictures, videos, and links to numerous web sites, visit http://www.tisv.be/mt/film.htm.

NOTES

_____

_____

_____

_____

_____

_____

_____

_____

_____

_____

Courtesy of Warner Press

JESUS
(5 BCE - 30 CE)
By Marshall Jenkins

Of Jesus' place in history, Jaroslav Pelikan wrote: "Regardless of what anyone may personally think or believe about him, Jesus of Nazareth has been the dominant figure in the history of Western culture for almost twenty centuries. If it were possible, with some sort of supermagnet, to pull up out of that history every scrap of metal bearing at least a trace of his name, how much would be left? It is from his birth that most of the human race dates its calendars, it is by his name that millions curse and in his name that millions pray" (Pelikan, 1985, 1). The gospels record precious little about Jesus' life prior to age 30 when his brief ministry started with his baptism, temptation in the desert, and mission statement (quoting the prophet Isaiah) delivered at the synagogue in his home town of Nazareth: "The Spirit of the Lord is upon me, because he has anointed me to bring good news to the poor. He has sent me to proclaim release to the captives and recovery of sight to the blind, to let the oppressed go free, to proclaim the year of the Lord's favor" (Luke 4:18-19).

> Those who want to save their life will lose it, and those who lose their life for my sake, and for the sake of the gospel, will save it (Mark 8:35).

Note: All scripture quotations are from the New Revised Standard Version Bible, Division of Christian Education of the National Council of Churches of Christ in the United States of America, 1989.

15

A rich man once asked Jesus, "What must I do to inherit eternal life?" (Mark 10:17). No one came closer to asking Jesus the modern question, "How shall I get a life?" With ample material comforts and plenty of reasons to feel good about himself, the rich man wanted more. Jesus offered a shocking response to the rich man, "Go, sell what you own, and give the money to the poor, and you will have treasure in heaven; then come, follow me" (Mark 10:21). As most of us would, the rich man walked away, dejected. Jesus did not ask literal poverty of everyone, for he gratefully accepted the provisions of some materially comfortable followers. But further examination of his life and teaching reveals how his response to the rich man answers the question, "How shall I get a life?" for all of us.

Examine Yourself

Socrates, not Jesus, said, "Know thyself." Jesus said, "Repent, and believe the good news" (Mark 1:15), a process that must begin with self-awareness. Like Socrates, Jesus challenged us to self-examination more by the method than the content of his teaching. On another day, in another place, Jesus said, "Let anyone among you who is without sin be the first to throw a stone" (John 8:7). Thus, he answered an angry band of religious leaders intent on using God's law to justify killing a woman caught in the act of adultery. Jesus forced them to see themselves as beneficiaries of God's mercy, dead men walking if not for grace. They dropped their stones and walked away.

Jesus promoted an examined life, but one of a very specific kind. Reading the classics, undergoing therapy, or passing a wilderness survival course promote useful self-examination in various ways, but not fully the way that Jesus had in mind. Jesus challenged his listeners to look at themselves with brutal honesty. If you look into your heart and find anger, you are no different than a murderer; if you find lust, you are no different than a philanderer. If your eye causes you to sin, pluck it out, and if your hand causes you to sin, chop it off. God allows no loopholes in judgments about divorce and perjury, and when God tells you to love, God makes no exceptions for vengeance or retribution (Matthew 5:21-48). No one can live up to these standards. Yet, Jesus confronted us with them to help us get past our egos and master the single most difficult spiritual challenge of all: accepting and giving undeserved love.

Obey God's Commandments

In his time, Jesus was a radical, not a rebel. A rebel scraps the old rules and writes new ones. A radical reads the old rules and, finding them neglected and trivialized, asserts them anew.

> Do not think that I have come to abolish the law or the prophets; I have come not to abolish but to fulfill....Whoever breaks one of the least of these commandments, and teaches others to do the same will be called least in the kingdom of heaven; but whoever does them and teaches them will be called great in the kingdom of heaven (Matthew 5:17, 19-20).

As the true radical, he could not resist concluding, "For I tell you, unless your righteousness exceeds that of the Scribes and Pharisees, you will never enter the kingdom of heaven" (Matthew 5:17,19-20).

Jesus was a good Jew who followed the laws of the ancient Hebrews set forth by the Torah, which we find in the first five books of the Hebrew Bible (or Old Testament). The Ten Commandments and specific cultic and social laws appear in various parts of these books, and good Jews take seriously the interpretation and application of these maxims in daily life.

But the Torah also contains epic stories of creation, rebellion, liberation, journey, war, romance, cunning, savagery, and civilization. Reading the law meant not only reading rules, but observing human lives lived in relation to God and gaining from the stories a deeper understanding of where the community's life and one's own life fit into God's plan. As a radical, Jesus saw the Scribes, Sadducees, and Pharisees—the religious authorities of the time— as having reduced the law to burdensome rules with little relation to the spirit of their original intent. Getting a life for a good Jew meant falling more and more deeply in love with God, not blindly obeying laws.

> "Which commandment is the first of all?" asked a scribe, and Jesus answered, "The first is, 'Hear O Israel: the Lord our God, the Lord is one; you shall love the Lord your God with all your heart, and with all your soul, and with all your mind, and with all your strength.' The second is this, 'You shall love your neighbor as yourself.' There is no other commandment greater than these" (Mark 12:28b-31).

Thus followed a rare moment of concord between Jesus and one of the religious authorities. Both understood that the love of neighbor completes the love of God and that such integrated love summarizes the whole Jewish law.

17

For the good Jew, obedience to God's commandments has everything to do with freedom. We think too easily of the "Thou shalt nots" as limits to freedom, and that they are. They limit freedom like roots limit a flower to one place. Without roots, the flower dies, bereft of soil and nourishment. Likewise, without obedience to God's commandments, we lose our freedom.

The most precious freedom is not freedom to do as we please, but freedom to love. If we only exercised the freedom to do as we please, we imprison ourselves in self-seeking obsessions, isolate ourselves, and trample the freedoms of others. Moreover, freedom to do as we please will never satisfy our deepest desire, the desire for love, because love in God's world only comes in the joyous, messy, painful business of committed relationships that mirror God's committed relationship with us. Gratitude for God's love makes the good life possible. Such gratitude leads to living in God's reality, a reality defined by committed relationships and freedom to love, not by impersonal laws and hedonic calculations (see John 8:31-36).

Jesus Loves You

Sitting quietly with my newborn son, Philip, in my arms, I take a deep breath. As a first time father, surprises come with every moment. For instance, I never anticipated the trajectory of his urine the first time I changed a wet diaper. I never counted the infinite ways he might harm himself by putting things in his mouth and exploring the great unknown. I never knew a heart could enlarge to near bursting until I saw him cry.

But I who never sang for anyone without an accompanying crowd to drown me out, faced with fear and trembling the challenge of singing my son to sleep for the first time. Searching my memory for a children's song, I remembered only one, and I sang it:

Jesus loves me, this I know,
For the Bible tells me so.
Little ones to him belong.
They are weak, but he is strong.
Yes, Jesus loves me.
Yes, Jesus loves me.
Yes, Jesus loves me,
For the Bible tells me so.

Karl Barth once said that if he had to summarize the Christian message in a few words, he would sing that song. So I knew I wasn't feeding my kid junk. I still sing it to him.

As a follower of Jesus, I naturally want him to know that Jesus loves him every step along the way, even as love becomes more confusing, painful, and exhilarating with each stage of his life. Like any parent, I want him to have a life, a good life. It might seem like enough to abstract wise maxims about righteous living from Jesus' teachings and encourage him by example and instruction to apply them. But Jesus himself insists on more than that.

> On the night when he was betrayed, [Jesus] took a loaf of bread, and when he had given thanks, he broke it and said, 'This is my body that is for you. Do this in remembrance of me.' In the same way he took the cup also, after supper, saying, 'This cup is the new covenant in my blood. Do this, as often as you drink it in remembrance of me' (I Corinthians 11:23-25).

Ever since that night, Christians have repeated the ritual to remember him, to mark a covenant with God and with the body and blood of a man who died for love. To get a life, one must accept Jesus' radical love, a suffering, dying, and eternally living love.

Join the Poor

Material goods possess us—homes, cars, wine cellars, objects to which we attach status. Jesus advocated a willingness to give it all away. Maybe you'll get it all back, but more likely, you'll get something better and more bountiful back. Whatever you get, you'll be free.

As Jesus said, "Come, you that are blessed by my Father, inherit the kingdom prepared for you from the foundation of the world; for I was hungry and you gave me some food, I was thirsty and you gave me something to drink, I was a stranger and you welcomed me, I was sick and you took care of me, I was in prison and you visited me....Truly I tell you, just as you did it to one of the least of these who are members of my family, you did it to me" (Matthew 25:34-36, 40). To get a life, give. Give not to achieve your own righteousness, but to have another moment with Christ.

Seek First the Kingdom of God

Where suffering and love meet, the fog lifts, and we see the splendor of God's reign all about us. The central theme of Jesus' teaching—indeed of his ministry—was the kingdom of God.

Jesus never defined the kingdom. He showed us snapshots called parables. The kingdom of God is like yeast, morsels literally blended and lost in dough; yet, it makes the bread rise, fill the air with sweetness, and feeds us until we're satisfied (Matthew 13:33). The kingdom of God is like a pearl found in a field that so excites a merchant that he sells all he has and buys the field just to have that one thing (Matthew 13:44). It is like the rare seed that falls not on rocks or walkways but on good soil unhindered by weeds or feeding birds, the rare seed that endures and dies to bear fruit (Matthew 13:1-23).

Jesus provided evidence of the kingdom every time he healed the blind, infirm, and dying. He brought love and healing even to those plagued by doubt or demons. He showed the order of the kingdom with his repeated refrain that the first will be last. The kingdom is a work in progress, the final home for the living. Opening our eyes to it, stepping into it, and living in its order means that we need worry no more than the birds about finding food, no more than the lilies about clothes. "Strive first for the kingdom of God and his righteousness, and all these things will be given to you as well" (Matthew 6:33).

The Paradox

When Jesus told the rich man to relinquish all his material props, he told him to give up his life as he knew it. He promised him a new life. To this particular man, trapped in his world of inadequate answers as the void sucked his soul away, Jesus offered his prescription based on a paradox that he repeated and paraphrased often: Those who lose their lives will save it, and those who seek to save their lives will lose it.

His death and resurrection elevated this paradox to something more than a wise aphorism. Those events still frame the hope for his followers. In a flash of clarity his outspoken disciple, Peter, answered Jesus' question, "Who do you say that I am?" with the first Christian confession: "You are the Messiah." Yet within moments, Peter committed the first confessional lapse when he argued against the necessity of Jesus' persecution and death. "Get behind me, Satan!" Jesus roared, "For you are setting your mind not on divine things but on human things." Then to his disciples and everyone else in earshot, he elaborated: "If any want to become my followers, let them deny themselves and take up their cross and follow me. For those who want to save their life will lose it, and those who lose their life for my sake, and for the sake of the gospel, will save it. For what will it profit them to gain the whole world and forfeit their life?" (Mark 8:31-37).

All of Jesus' teachings culminate in the paradox of losing one's life to find it. The good life involves letting go of the lesser gods that prey on the anxieties that lead us to accumulate material wealth. We cling to these lesser gods and bet our lives on them because we can bottle, measure, name, and predict them. Deep down we know that they leave our souls restless, but the restlessness becomes comfortably familiar. Jesus said,

> Come to me, all you who are weary and are carrying heavy burdens, and I will give you rest. Take my yoke upon you, and learn from me; for I am gentle and humble in heart, and you will find rest for your souls. For my yoke is easy and my burden is light (Matthew 11:28-30).

Biographical Sketch

Jesus was a Jewish peasant from the rural town of Nazareth in Galilee. Born around 5 B.C., his life of approximately 33 years took place entirely during the *Pax Romana*, or "Roman peace," a dubious peace for occupied people like the Jews of Palestine. Little is recorded about his early life before beginning his public ministry at "about thirty years old" (Luke 3:23). The little information offered in Luke suggests that he was raised in a devout Jewish family and that he may have participated in his father's trade as a carpenter. His ministry consisted of itinerant teaching and miraculous healing, mostly in Galilee. While details of his educational background are unknown, the authority with which he taught is noted several times within the gospels, and even his foes referred to him with the rabbinical title, "Teacher." Twelve disciples constituted his core group of followers, although many more were probably considered his disciples in a broader sense.

Jesus apparently lived in poverty. "Foxes have holes, and birds of the air have nests; but the Son of Man has nowhere to lay his head" (Matthew

8:20). His ministry included constant antagonistic tension with official religious authorities. He frequently irritated these authorities with his challenges to Jewish law as they understood it (e.g., healing on the Sabbath) and his association with women and persons of ill repute. His relations with government authorities appear to range more widely from angry (referring to Herod as "that fox" in Luke 13:31-33) to warm (referring to a Roman centurion as one whose faith exceeds that of anyone in the region, Luke 7:1-10). The story of his crucifixion reflects his lowly status, but the story of his resurrection elevates him above the worldly. No figure in history has exercised greater cultural influence for longer (more than 2000 years and counting) in the West than Jesus.

Because of his enormous impact on life at the personal, social, and political levels, his life story has been the subject of intense scrutiny and debate. The four gospels that tell his story were not written primarily for historians, but for an ancient, marginalized church community that turned to these sources for sustenance during the exigencies of life together in an often hostile world. But the telling of the story of Jesus by these early churches constitutes the central creed of Christian churches to this day. In his first witness to Gentiles (non-Jews), Peter told the following story:

> I truly understand that God shows no partiality, but in every nation anyone who fears him and does what is right is acceptable to him. You know the message that he sent to the people of Israel, preaching peace by Jesus Christ—he is Lord of all. That message spread throughout Judea, beginning in Galilee after the baptism that John announced: How God anointed Jesus of Nazareth with the Holy Spirit and with power; how he went about doing good and healing all who were oppressed by the devil, for God was with him. We are witnesses to all that he did both in Judea and in Jerusalem. They put him to death by hanging him on a tree; but God raised him on the third day and allowed him to appear, not to all the people but to us who were chosen by God as witnesses, and who ate and drank with him after he rose from the dead. He commanded us to preach to the people and to testify that he is the one ordained by God as judge of the living and the dead. All the prophets testify about him that everyone who believes in him receives forgiveness of sins through his name (Acts 10:34-43).

When the Road is Smooth

Shortly after the encounter with the rich man, two disciples—James and John—apparently feeling rather accomplished as disciples—asked Jesus for a privileged place in the kingdom. Jesus saw the seeds of the religious authorities' folly in their request, the pride and tyranny of those who hoard spiritual status. He reminded them that a place in the kingdom costs one's life, and he repeated the paradox: "Whoever wished to be great among you must be your servant, and whoever wishes to be first among you must be slave of all" (Mark 10:43-44).

To grow spiritually, you must get out of your comfort zone and begin serving humanity.

When the Road Gets Rocky

When circumstance turns against you, fear not, for God will provide what is needed.

Blessed are the poor in spirit, for theirs is the kingdom of heaven.

Blessed are those who mourn, for they will be comforted.

Blessed are the meek, for they will inherit the earth.

Blessed are those who hunger and thirst for righteousness, for they will be filled.

Blessed are the merciful, for they will receive mercy.

Blessed are the pure in heart, for they will see God.

Blessed are the peacemakers, for they will be called children of God.

Blessed are those who are persecuted for righteousness' sake, for theirs is the kingdom of heaven.

Blessed are you when people revile you and persecute you and utter all kinds of evil against you falsely on my account.

Rejoice and be glad, for your reward is great in heaven, for in the same way they persecuted the prophets who were before you (Matthew 5:3-12).

When You Encounter a Dragon in the Middle of the Road

Love the dragon and pray for him.

Love your enemies and pray for those who persecute you, so that you may be children of your Father who is in heaven; for he makes his sun rise on the evil and on the good, and sends rain on the righteous and unrighteous (Matthew 5:44-45).

The Crux: Jesus' Advice for Getting a Life

1. Love God with all your heart, mind, soul, and strength. Love your neighbor as yourself. Do not separate these two commandments.
2. Honestly examine yourself for ways that you separate yourself from God and how you elevate yourself or anything else to the status of a god. Ask for God's forgiveness. No one gets beyond the need to do this regularly.
3. Accept undeserved love.
4. Give undeserved love.
5. As a fellow sufferer, minister to the suffering of those around you. Expect Jesus' presence in the encounter.
6. Even amid trials and adversity, be attentive to signs of God's loving reign within you and around you. No part of your world or your life is separate from God's concern.
7. Through scripture reading, prayer, and relationships with other people of faith, discern God's commands and obey them. This will bring you more freedom, not less.
8. Participate in a community of faith. Faith demands to be shared, and it is too fragile for any of us to sustain alone.
9. Lose your life to find it: Even as God created much for us to enjoy, one must be willing to lose everything to enjoy anything freely.
10. Do not worry about getting a life. Expect God to provide it, and let God guide you on a lifelong journey of discerning your life's meaning. Pay attention.

In a Nutshell

Two sayings of Jesus sum up his prescription for getting a life:

One of the scribes... asked [Jesus], "Which commandment is the first of all?" Jesus answered, "The first is, 'Hear, O Israel, the Lord our God, the Lord is one; you shall love the Lord your God with all your heart, and with all your soul, and with all your mind, and with all your strength.' The second is this, 'You shall love your neighbor as yourself'" (Mark 12:28-31).

"Those who want to save their life will lose it, and those who lose their life for my sake and for the sake of the gospel will save it" (Mark 8:35).

The Wisdom of Jesus

On Money
No one can serve two masters; for a slave will either hate the one and love the other, or be devoted to one and despise the other. You cannot serve God and wealth (Matthew 6:24).

On Leisure
Enter through the narrow gate; for the gate is wide and the road is easy that leads to destruction, and there are many who take it. For the gate is narrow and the road is hard that leads to life, and there are few who find it (Matthew 7:13-14).

On Virtue
No good tree bears bad fruit, nor again does a bad tree bear good fruit; for each tree is known by its own fruit. Figs are not gathered from thorns, nor are grapes picked from a bramble bush. The good person out of the good treasure of the heart produces good, and the evil person out of the evil treasure produces evil; for it is out of the abundance of the heart that the mouth speaks (Luke 6:43-45).

On Finding Bliss
Do not be afraid, little flock, for it is your Father's good pleasure to give you the kingdom. Sell your possessions, and give alms. Make purses for yourselves that do not wear out, an unfailing treasure in heaven, where no thief comes near and no moth destroys. For where your treasure is, there your heart will be also (Luke 12:32-34).

On Children and Religion
Let the little children come to me; do not stop them; for it is to such as these that the kingdom of God belongs. Truly I tell you, whoever does not receive the kingdom of God as a little child will never enter it (Mark 10:14-15).

On Truth

If you love me, you will keep my commandments. And I will ask the Father, and he will give you another Advocate, to be with you forever. This is the Spirit of truth, whom the world cannot receive, because it neither sees him nor knows him. You know him, because he abides with you, and he will be in you (John 14:15-17).

Important Dates (all estimates)

5 BCE — Born in Bethlehem of Judea (Luke 2:1-40)
7 CE — Extended visit with teachers in Jerusalem temple (Luke 2:41-52)
26 CE — Beginning of ministry (Luke 3:23)
30 CE — Crucifixion, resurrection, and ascension

References and Resources

Borg, M. J. 1987. *Jesus: A New Vision.* San Francisco: HarperSanFrancisco.
Bornkamm, G. 1960. *Jesus of Nazareth.* New York: Harper & Row, Publishers.
Brown, R. 1997. *An Introduction to the New Testament.* New York: Doubleday.
Drane, J. 1986. *Introducing the New Testament.* San Francisco: HarperSanFrancisco.
Hunter, A. M. 1965. *A Pattern for Life.* Philadelphia: The Westminster Press.
Jenkins, J. M. 2000. *A Wakeful Faith: Spiritual Practice in the Real World.* Nashville, TN: Upper Room Books.
Kung, H. 1976. *On Being a Christian.* Garden City, NY: Doubleday & Company, Inc.
Nineham, D.E. 1963. *Saint Mark.* New York: Penguin Books.
Pelikan, J. 1985. *Jesus Through the Centuries.* New York: Harper & Row.
Perkins, P. 1990. *Jesus as Teacher.* New York: Cambridge University Press.

NOTES

A/P World Wide Photos

28

MARTIN LUTHER KING, JR.

(1929-1968)

By Ben DeVan

Martin Luther King, Jr., was the conscience of his generation. A southerner and a black man, he gazed on the great wall of segregation and saw that the power of love could bring it down. From the pain and exhaustion of his fight to free people from the bondage of separation and injustice, he offered a dream of what America could be.

Even during his final days, he was working to build a world where the poorest and humblest among us could enjoy the fulfillment of the promises of our founding fathers. His life informed us, and his dreams sustain us yet. (Adapted from the posthumous award of the Presidential Medal of Freedom, July 4, 1977.)

> And when we allow freedom to ring, when we let it ring from every village and hamlet, from every state and city, we will be able to speed up that day when all God's children—black men and white men, Jews and Gentiles, Catholics and Protestants—will be able to join hands and to sing in the words of the old Negro spiritual, "Free at last, free at last; thank God almighty we are free at last" (King, 1986, 220).

Martin Luther King, Jr., is one of the greatest Americans of the twentieth century and one of the most potent rhetoricians of all time. His fight against segregation, injustice, and racial inequality changed the face of American society forever. A Baptist minister who received his Doctor of Philosophy from Boston University, King has inspired numerous books, articles, films, documentaries, paintings, and monuments. "By marching, singing, praying, and suffering, Martin Luther King let America out of the prison of legal segregation" (Lincoln, 1970, 173).

Major Influences

King was a voracious reader as an undergraduate, seminary student, and doctoral candidate. The work of three men particularly influenced his philosophy of justice and creative extremism—Henry David Thoreau, Mohandas Gandhi, and Jesus Christ.

King first came into contact with Thoreau's *Essay On Civil Disobedience* in college and "was fascinated by the possibility of refusing to cooperate with an evil system" (Walton, 1971, 41). King was so deeply moved that he reread the work several times (Walton, 1971). He was particularly taken with Thoreau's notion of a "peaceable revolution."

This "peaceable revolution" was personified by Mohandas Gandhi, who led India into independence from Great Britain using the concept of "non-violent" nationalism or passive resistance. Gandhi maintained, "I believe in the doctrine of non-violence as a weapon of the weak. I believe in the doctrine of non-violence as a weapon of the strongest. I believe that a man is the strongest soldier for daring to die unarmed" (Seldes, 1996, 172). According to King, Gandhi "was the first person in history to lift the love ethic of Jesus above mere interaction with individuals" (Walton, 1971, 43).

An even greater influence on King than Gandhi was Jesus Christ. King contended, "It was Jesus of Nazareth that stirred the Negroes to protest with the creative weapon of love" (King, 1986, 18). Jesus' *Sermon on the Mount* (Matthew 5-7) with its emphasis on humility, forgiveness, and revolutionary compassion, provided the inspiration for King's nonviolent approach (Walton, 1971). On Jesus, King wrote,

> Jesus eloquently affirmed from the cross a higher law. He knew that the old eye-for-an-eye philosophy would leave everyone blind. He did not seek to overcome evil with evil. He overcame evil with

good. Although crucified by hate, he responded with aggressive love. What a magnificent lesson! Generations will rise and fall; men will continue to worship the god of revenge and bow before the altar of retaliation; but ever and again this noble lesson of Calvary will be a nagging reminder that only goodness can drive out evil and only love can conquer hate (King, 1981, 42).

Through Jesus' vision, King saw hope for America and the world. In his essay "Where Do We Go From Here?" King explicated his plan for changing the structure of American society. He wanted to change America from "a dream as yet unfulfilled" to a "land where men of all races, of all nationalities and of all creeds can live together as brothers" (King, 1986, 208). "I have a dream," King envisaged, "my four little children will one day live in a nation where they will not be judged by the color of their skin but by the content of their character" (219).

King embraced the Christian doctrine of loving his enemies, even under the most desperate conditions. "With this faith," King asserted, "we will be able to hew out of the mountain of despair a stone of hope. With this faith we will be able to transform the jangling discords of our nation into a beautiful sympathy of brotherhood" (King, 1986, 219). King did not believe brotherhood occurred without effort and sacrifice. The trail to the dream must be blazed and the moment for blazing seized.

Seizing the Moment

One of the greatest obstacles King experienced on the road to freedom surfaced from well-meaning "moderates" who admonished King to "just wait and be patient" (King, 1986, 213). They rationalized that the goals he desired for justice and integration would gradually come to pass within twenty to two hundred years. King, however, believed that a laissez-faire attitude based on the notion that somehow time would inevitably cure all ills was "a tragic misconception" (296). Progress would not be made by doing nothing. King was eloquent in his rebuttals as to why justice could not wait:

The time is always ripe to do right,
Justice too long delayed is justice denied,
I wonder at men who dare to feel that they have some paternalistic right to set the timetable for another man's liberation (King, 1986, 296, 292, 335).

Convinced of the urgency for civil rights, King promoted courage over caution, action over indecision, and discussion over silence (King 1986, 221, 243, 231). He knew that freedom would never be voluntarily "given up by the oppressor; it must be demanded by the oppressed" (292).

Continuity of Actions and Words

One of King's frustrations with politicians of his day was that they seemed to "so often have a high blood pressure of words and an anemia of deeds" (King, 1986, 198). King observed a schizophrenic personality in America, one whose practices belied the principles on which the country was founded (208).

Rather than give lip service to the rights of life, liberty, and the pursuit of happiness, King thought it was the right of every American to live them. Although King condemned the violence of his oppressors, he also railed against the "appalling silence and indifference of good people" (King, 1986, 275). Confrontation of evil was absolutely necessary for the continued survival of a just American society. King wanted us to become "not detached spectators, but involved participants" in seeing that justice was done in America and throughout the world (215).

A Brotherhood of Mankind

King's belief in God and the solidarity of the human family spurred his desire for integration (King, 1986, 121). While seeking desegregation legally, King sought integration practically. He knew that desegregation was a necessary first step if true integration were to be achieved (123). King spurned the idea of "physical proximity without spiritual affinity"…where elbows are together but hearts are apart (118). King's dream of integration included togetherness in doing and being; sharing in responsibility, love, and power. King counseled his fellow African-Americans "Let us be dissatisfied until that day when nobody will shout 'White Power!'—when nobody will shout 'Black Power!'—but everybody will talk about God's power and human power" (251).

All people have "dignity and worth of human personality" (King, 1986, 215) because every human being is made in the image of God and beloved by God. This preciousness of people as mirrors of God's image and objects of divine love shatters convenient categories seeking to measure human significance by race, intellect, or social position.

King believed that all life was interrelated, that the destinies of all humans were inextricably interwoven (King, 1986, 210). His sincere hope was that all citizens of earth would come to share in a fair and gentle brotherhood of mankind. King wrote, "We must all learn to live together as brothers, or we will all perish together as fools" (209).

On Love

For King, love was the highest virtue, the most essential ingredient of the good life, and the defining principle of ultimate reality. King differentiated love from "emotional bosh" and liking.

> It is pretty difficult to like some people. Like is sentimental and it is pretty difficult to like someone bombing your home; it is pretty difficult to like congressmen who spend all of their time trying to defeat civil rights. But Jesus says love them, and love is greater than like (King, 1987, 37).

In contrast to mere "liking," King defines love (as the *Bible* does) as the Greek word *Agape*, a redemptive spirit of good will that seeks nothing in return. "Love is the only force on earth that can be dispensed or received in an extreme manner, without any qualifications, without any harm to the giver or the receiver" (King, 1986, 356). King's idea of love was neither sentimental nor weak, but "the supreme unifying principle of life" (242).

The Power of Nonviolent Resistance

King's respect for the dignity of the self, and his philosophy of agape love undergirded his method of protest, nonviolent resistance. Nonviolence attacks the forces of evil rather than the people caught up in those forces. King's philosophy of nonviolence, "the willingness to be the recipient of violence while never inflicting violence upon another" (King, 1986, 336-337) has perhaps been the most criticized of his views. For King, nonviolence was a weapon fabricated of love, a "sword that heals," transforming both the oppressor and the oppressed. Nonviolence does not attempt to humiliate the oppressor, rather it seeks to win his or her understanding and acknowledgement of what is morally right (10).

In the film *Do The Right Thing*, director Spike Lee included the following passage from King:

> Violence as a way of achieving racial justice is both impractical and immoral. It is impractical because it is a descending spiral ending in destruction for all. The old law of an eye for an eye leaves everybody blind. It is immoral because it seeks to humiliate the opponent rather than win his understanding! It seeks to annihilate rather than convert. Violence is immoral because it thrives on hatred rather than love. It destroys community and makes brotherhood impossible. It leaves society in monologue rather than dialogue. Violence ends by defeating itself. It creates bitterness in the survivors and brutality in the destroyers (Lee, 1988; also King, 1987, 73).

King required that every protestor who marched with him receive nonviolent training. His fellow protestors had to sign a pledge which required, among other things, to "refrain from the violence of fist, tongue, or heart" (Ansbro, 1982). Not only did King forbid his colleagues to physically injure their opponents, he continually quoted Booker T. Washington who said, "Let no man pull you so low as to make you hate him" (King, 1986, 20). King's interpretation of nonviolence was founded upon Christian ethics and "on the conviction that the universe is on the side of justice" (9).

> The phrase "passive resistance" often gives the false impression that this is a sort of "do-nothing method" in which the resister quietly and passively accepts evil. But nothing is further from the truth. For while the nonviolent resister is passive in the sense that he is not physically aggressive toward his opponent, his mind and emotions are always active, constantly seeking to persuade his opponent that he is wrong. The method is passive physically but strongly active spiritually. It is not passive nonresistance to evil; it is active nonviolent resistance to evil (King, 1986, 18).

Biographical Sketch

Martin Luther King, Jr., was born in Atlanta, Georgia, on January 15, 1929. His parents were Michael (later known as Martin) King, a Baptist minister, and Alberta Williams King, a schoolteacher. King's brother and maternal grandfather were also Baptist ministers. At age fifteen King entered Morehouse College. He graduated with a B.A. in Sociology and was ordained at nineteen. King then entered Pennsylvania's Crozer Theological Seminary where he was elected student body president. Crozer introduced King to the ideas of Gandhi, Rauschenbusch (propagator of the "social gospel," a movement that sought to create the Kingdom of God on earth through social and economic reform), and other influential thinkers. After graduating from Crozer first in his class, King earned a Ph.D. in Systematic (or Philosophical) Theology from Boston University. While at Boston he met his wife Coretta Scott of Alabama, who was studying at the New England Conservatory of Music. They had four children—Yolanda Denise, Martin Luther III, Dexter, and Bernice Albertine.

King accepted his first pastorate at Dexter Avenue Baptist Church in Montgomery, Alabama, where he helped organize bus boycotts inspired by the racial injustices suffered by Rosa Parks and others. King and other black ministers founded the Southern Christian Leadership Conference (SCLC) in 1957 as a base of operation for the Civil Rights movement and a national platform from which to speak. Through the SCLC King lectured, conferred with heads of state, and visited Ghana and India where he met with India's prime minister and successor of Gandhi, Jawaharlal Nehru.

King's leadership in the civil rights movement climaxed from 1960 to 1965 when he accepted a pastoral position at his father's church in Atlanta and participated and instigated creative forms of non-violent protest such as sit-ins, freedom bus rides, and marches. In the spring of 1963, King launched a massive campaign in Birmingham, Alabama, a city that epitomized racial prejudice in the south. The Birmingham police, under the leadership of Chief Eugene "Bull" Connor, arrested hundreds of demonstrators using attack dogs, tear gas, electric cattle prods, and fire hoses as the nation watched on television with horror. A black church was bombed, killing four girls attending Sunday school, and King was thrown into the Birmingham City Jail where he wrote his famous "Letter from Birmingham City Jail." This letter is probably the magnum opus of King's personal, political, and philosophical thought on injustice, love, and creative protest.

On August 28, 1963, King spoke at the historic "March on Washington," the greatest civil rights demonstration in the history of America. In front of the Lincoln Memorial, King delivered his prophetic "I

Have a Dream" speech to approximately 250,000 marchers. In 1964, King became the youngest recipient of the Nobel Peace Prize and was named "Man of the Year" by *Time* magazine, the first black American ever so honored. It would seem to this writer that every human being would benefit from reading, and rereading, this "Letter from Birmingham City Jail" and the "I Have a Dream" speech.

Following the March on Washington, President Lyndon B. Johnson signed the Civil Rights Act of 1964 banning discrimination based on color, race, national origin, religion, or sex by programs receiving funds from the federal government. It also forced desegregation of public facilities including parks, hotels, restaurants, and schools. After further demonstrations (the most famous occurring in Selma, Alabama) the Voting Rights Act of 1965 was passed providing federal protection for blacks who wished to vote.

In 1967, King began opposing the Vietnam War. He felt that the war effort committed physical, spiritual, and psychological atrocities against both Americans and Vietnamese while requiring billions of dollars that could better be spent in a war against poverty, ill health, and lack of education. During this time, King's attention began focusing on rights, justice, and alleviating hardships faced by poor people of all races. Amidst a campaign for sanitation workers in Memphis, Tennessee, King was shot and killed on April 4, 1968. America mourned and more than 100,000 attended King's funeral in Atlanta. His tombstone was engraved with "Free at last, Free at last, thank God Almighty I'm free at last."

When the Road is Smooth

In his adult life King rarely knew a moment when the road was smooth. When he advanced the cause of justice in one area, he soon discovered another place of need. In his "Letter from the Birmingham City Jail" King wrote, "Injustice anywhere is a threat to justice everywhere." (King, 1986, 290). Even though King's life was harried and challenging, he carved out time for family, prayer, and meditation.

> Every day when I'm at home I break from the office for dinner and try to spend a few hours with the children before I return to the office for some night work. And on Tuesdays when I'm not out of town, I don't go to the office. I keep this for my quiet day of reading and silence and meditation, and an entire evening with Mrs. King and the children (King, 1986, 372).

When the Road Gets Rocky

King reflected much about how to respond when the road gets rocky.
I must confess my friends; the road ahead will not always be
smooth. There will still be rocky places of frustration and mean-
dering points of bewilderment. There will be inevitable setbacks
here and there…we must walk on in the days ahead with an auda-
cious faith in the future…let us remember that there is a creative
force in this universe, working to pull down the gigantic mountains
of evil, a power that is able to make a way out of no way and transform dark yesterdays into bright tomorrows (King, 1986, 251-252).

People are often surprised to learn that I am an optimist. They know
how often I have been jailed, how frequently the days and nights
have been filled with frustration and sorrow, how bitter and dangerous are my adversaries. They expect these experiences to hard-
en me into a grim and desperate man. They fail, however, to perceive the sense of affirmation generated by the challenge of
embracing struggle and surmounting obstacles. They have no com-
prehension of the strength that comes from faith in God and man.
It is possible for me to falter, but I am profoundly secure in my
knowledge that God loves us; he has not worked out a design for
our failure (King, 1986, 314).

But I know, somehow, that only when it is dark enough, can you see
the stars (King, 1986, 314).

When You Encounter a Dragon in the Middle of the Road

Learn from the dragon

Compassion and nonviolence help us to see the enemy's point of
view, to hear his questions, to know his assessment of ourselves.
For from his view we may indeed see the basic weaknesses of our
own condition, and if we are mature, we may learn and grow and
profit from the wisdom of the brothers who are called opposition
(King, 1987, 78).

Respect the dragon
> In the course of respecting the discipline of the nonviolent way, the Negro has learned that he must respect the adversary who inflicts the system upon him and he develops the capacity to hate segregation but to love the segregationist. He learns in the midst of his determined efforts to destroy the system that has shackled him so long, that a commitment to Nonviolence demands that he respect the personhood of his opponent (King, 1986, 125).

Persuade the dragon peacefully
> Nonviolent resistance does not seek to humiliate the opponent, but to win his friendship and understanding (King, 1986, 7).

If the dragon will not be persuaded, move forward creatively, confidently and nonviolently
> When evil men plot, good men must plan. When evil men burn and bomb, good men must build and bind. When evil men shout ugly words of hatred, good men must commit themselves to the glories of love. Where evil men would seek to perpetuate unjust status quo, good men must seek to bring into being a real order of justice (King, 1987, 51).

The Crux

> So I say to you, seek God and discover Him and make Him a power in your life. Without Him all of our efforts turn to ashes and our sunrises into darkest nights. Without Him, life is a meaningless drama with the decisive scenes missing. But with Him we are able to rise from the fatigue of despair to the buoyancy of hope. With Him we are able to rise from the midnight of desperation to the daybreak of joy. St. Augustine was right—we were made for God and we will be restless until we find rest in Him.
>
> Love yourself, if that means rational, healthy, and moral self-interest. You are commanded to do that. That is the length of life. Love your neighbor as yourself. You are commanded to do that. That is the breadth of life. But never forget that there is a first and even greater commandment, 'Love the Lord thy God with all thy heart and all thy soul and all thy mind.' This is the height of life. And when you do this you live the complete life (King, 1987, 64).

In a Nutshell

I still believe that standing up for the truth of God is the greatest thing in the world. This is the end of life. The end of life is not to be happy. The end of life is not to achieve pleasure and avoid pain. The end of life is to do the will of God, come what may (King, 1986, 10).

If I can help somebody as I pass along, if I can cheer somebody with a word or song, if I can show somebody he's traveling wrong, then my living will not be in vain. If I can do my duty as a Christian ought, if I can bring salvation to a world once wrought, if I can spread the message as the master taught, then my living will not be in vain (King, 1986, 267).

The Wisdom of Martin Luther King Jr.

On Criticism
As Lincoln said, "If I answered all criticism, I'd have time for nothing else" (King, 1986, 248).

On Forgiveness
Forgiveness is not an occasional act; it is a permanent attitude (King, 1987, 23).

On Setting Goals
In order to answer the question, "where do we go from here"…we must first honestly recognize where we are now (King, 1986, 245).

On Leadership
Ultimately a genuine leader is not a searcher for consensus, but a molder of consensus (King, 1986, 277).

On Popularity
There comes a time when one must take the position that is neither safe nor politic nor popular, but he must do it because conscience tells him it is right (King, 1986, 276-277).

On Peace

True peace is not merely the absence of tension; it is the presence of justice (King, 1987, 83).

On Ministry

A minister cannot preach the glories of heaven while ignoring social conditions in his own community that cause men an earthly hell (King, 1986, 346).

On the Measure of a Human Being

The ultimate measure of a man is not where he stands in moments of comfort and convenience, but where he stands at times of challenge and controversy. The true neighbor will risk his position, his prestige and even his life for the welfare of others. In dangerous valleys and hazardous pathways, he will lift some bruised and beaten brother to a higher and more noble life (King, 1981, 35).

Important Dates

1929   Born to Martin and Alberta King of Atlanta.

1948   Graduates from Morehouse College and ordained a minister at age nineteen.

1951   Graduates from Crozer Theological Seminary.

1953   Marries Coretta Scott of Alabama.

1954   Begins first pastorate at Dexter Avenue Baptist Church in Montgomery.

1955   Completes Doctor of Philosophy in Philosophical Theology from Boston University.

1957   Assists in forming Southern Christian Leadership Conference and selected as its first president.

1958   Publishes first book, *Stride Toward Freedom*. Survived an attempted assassination by an allegedly insane elderly black woman.

1960   King accepts pastorate in his father's church, Ebenezer Baptist, in Atlanta.

1963   Major Civil Rights Campaign in Birmingham, Alabama. "Letter from Birmingham City Jail."

1963   "I Have a Dream" speech (Washington, D.C.) to 250,000 marchers.

1964   Named "Man of the Year" by *Time* magazine. Receives Nobel Peace Prize.

1965   Marches from Selma to Montgomery, Alabama, with 3,200 people.
1968   Assassinated in Memphis at the Lorraine Motel.
1983   U.S. Congress declares King's birthday a federal holiday.

References and Resources

Adler, R. B., & Rodman, G. 1997. *Understanding Human Communication*. Harcourt Brace College Publishers.
Ansbro, J. J. 1982. Martin Luther King, Jr. *The Making of a Mind*. New York: Orbis Books, Maryknoll.
Carson, C. 1998. *The Autobiography of Martin Luther King, Jr.* New York: IPM in Association with Warner Books.
Haugen, G. 1999. *Good News About Injustice*. Downers Grove, IL: InterVarsity Press.
King, C. S. 1987. *The Words of Martin Luther King, Jr.* New York: Newmarket Press.
King, M. L., Jr. 1986. *A Testament of Hope: The Essential Writings and Speeches of Martin Luther King, Jr.* (J. M. Washington, Ed.). San Francisco: HarperSanFrancisco.
King, M. L., Jr. 2000. *The Papers of Martin Luther King, Jr.* London, England: University of California Press, Ltd.
King, M. L., Jr. 1981. *Strength to Love*. Philadelphia: Fortress Press.
Lee, S. (Writer/Director). 1988. *Do the Right Thing* [Motion picture]. United States: Universal Pictures.
Lincoln, C. E. 1970. *Martin Luther King, Jr.: A Profile*. New York: Hill and Wang: a division of Farrar, Straus and Giroux.
Lischer, R. 1995. *The Preacher King*. New York: Oxford University Press.
Oates, S. B. 1982. *Let the Trumpet Sound: The Life of Martin Luther King, Jr.* New York: Harper & Row Publishers.
Seldes, G. ed. 1996. *The Great Thoughts* (Rev. Ed.). New York: Ballantine Books.
Walton, H., Jr. 1971. *The Political Philosophy of Martin Luther King, Jr.* Westport, Connecticut: Greenport Publishing Co.
Yancey, P. 2001. *Soul Survivor*. New York: Doubleday.

NOTES

Photo of Joseph Campbell used with the permission of the Joseph Campbell Foundation (www.jcf.org).

JOSEPH CAMPBELL
(1904-1987)
By Robert Baines

Joseph Campbell was one of the world's foremost authorities on mythology. He spent his life studying the cultures of the planet, examining their myths and rituals, and extracting the principles that unify them. Campbell did not limit himself to scientific cataloging or narrow academic analysis. Rather, he viewed mythology as each culture's blueprint for the road to God and to individual fulfillment. Campbell documented mythology's profound influence on philosophy, art, religion, and music. Unlike most academics of the time that focused upon the differences among cultures, Campbell identified and expounded upon commonalities. He distilled the principles of mythology that tie civilization together as one. In the rituals of tribes in the Congo, the sonnets of Lao-tse, the arguments of Aquinas, and the strange details of Eskimo fairy tales, Joe found "one, shape-shifting yet marvelously constant story" (Campbell, 1949, 3).

About mythology, Campbell said, "My favorite definition of mythology: other people's religion. My favorite definition of religion: misunderstanding of mythology" (Campbell and Kennedy, 2001, 111). Campbell was uninterested in the mass market kind of life; he was more interested in using mythology to help individuals find their unique destiny. "Follow your bliss" became a favorite saying of Campbell's and was a popular mantra among his many followers during the late twentieth century.

The dark night of the soul comes just before revelation when everything is lost, and all seems darkness, then comes the new life and
all that is needed (Campbell and Osbon, 1991, 39).

Choosing Bliss or the Wasteland

Bliss is not an empty-headed contentment that comes with a second
glass of wine or the momentary delight of your favorite television show. Bliss
is deeper and more enduring, "a soothing light of satisfaction radiating from
deep in your soul" (Campbell and Osbon, 1991, 181). It's the best that's in
you. If you are not sure about what your bliss might look like, consider what
you loved to do as a child before you decided to get practical.

To reach your potential and have the deepest fulfillment, follow what
makes you glow—your bliss. If you surrender to your bliss, your path will be
revealed. When the path appears foreboding; when you have no support or
encouragement from those around you; when circumstances turn against you;
you must trust your instincts and remain on track. Only by discovering your
bliss, then seeking it with all your might, will you realize your destiny.

Of course, it is easy to become engulfed in the daily trials of living
and to neglect the soul. Over time, you may have lost sight of what you love,
what used to make life worth living. If you are unsure about your bliss, Joe
suggests that you find a secluded, quiet space where you can think and reflect
without interruption. While you inhabit your space, do not read the newspaper or turn on the television; do not think about unpaid bills or problems at
work. Instead, reflect upon who you are and spend time doing the things you
love to do. Although a revelation may not arise immediately, if you regularly
devote time to your sacred space, an answer will come. Return to your sacred
space to rejuvenate and contemplate, "where there is a spring of ambrosia—
a joy that comes from inside, not something external that puts joy into you—
a place that lets you experience your own will and your intention and your
own wish so that...the Kingdom is there" (Campbell and Osbon, 1991, 180).

> Your bliss is your rapture, your gift, your unique purpose. Once you
> find it, you must exercise the will to follow the rocky and some-
> times painful path where it leads. You enter the forest at the dark-
> est point where there is no path. Where there is a way or path it is
> somebody else's path. You are not on your own path. If you follow
> someone else's way, you are not going to realize your potential
> (Campbell and Osbon, 1991, 22).

Anyone can "go with the flow" of popular wisdom and be led by friends, experts, or parents towards rational ends. However, these ends might have nothing to do with what you want to do. Each of us has the power to create the kind of life we want. Deciding not to choose is certainly an option, although it is the coward's way. Courage is required to live life like you think it should be lived. Taking a well-worn path is easy, but that is tantamount to surrendering to the Wasteland.

> The majority of my friends are living Wasteland lives. In teaching, you have people who haven't come into the Wasteland yet. They're at the point of making the decision whether they're going to follow the way of their own zeal—the star that's dawned for them—or do what daddy and mother and friends want them to do. The adventure is always in the dark forest, and there's something perilous about it (Campbell, Toms, Maher, and Biggs, 1990, 66-67).

The Hero and the Quest

The fundamental myth underlying most cultures is the one of the hero. Joe believed that every individual must take his/her own adventure. The hero must leave the safety of the home and the network of loved ones, and venture into the unknown. While in unchartered territory, the hero confronts a shadow presence (fears and desires, sometimes in the form of a dragon) and surmounts challenges all along the way. The hero either slays the dragon or dies trying. "The very cave you are afraid to enter turns out to be the source of what you are looking for. The damned thing in the cave that was so dreaded has become the center" (Campbell and Cousineau, 1990, 24).

In this long, difficult, and painful journey, the hero discovers new knowledge, which he/she brings back to the home and family. The hero discovers his identity and how he differs from parents only by leaving the safety of the home and going on the quest. As with chivalrous heroes in medieval times, the hero participates in the quest with passion, quiet dignity, love for his fellow humans, and a heart full of hope. He does not go on the quest for reasons of revenge, disappointment, or anger.

Did Campbell Follow his Own Advice?

Joseph Campbell followed his bliss and had a full, interesting life. One of the most impressive aspects about Joe's life is how often he managed to say, "No," when he was asked to do something he didn't believe in. He never worked solely for money. As a boy wonder at Columbia, Joe quit the Ph.D. program when he determined a doctorate was no longer part of his bliss. Instead, he moved to a cottage in the woods near Woodstock, NY, read books, and played in a jazz band for several years. Then, he rolled out to California, hung out with John Steinbeck and Ed Ricketts, fell in love with Carol Steinbeck (John's wife), and played around with writing fiction. At the time, he had no agenda other than just wandering around and thinking. "Rambling is a chance to sniff things out and somehow get a sense of where you feel you can settle" (Campbell and Osbon, 1991, 68).

When he finished reading some of the books he wanted to read, a teaching position mysteriously opened up at Sarah Lawrence University. The job at Sarah Lawrence allowed him to teach for three days a week, leaving him four days to pursue his passion of uncovering the links among the world's civilizations. He taught at Sarah Lawrence for almost thirty years, and then followed his bliss into publishing and speaking.

The works of Joseph Campbell have had remarkable influence on the thinking of filmmakers, artists, dancers, novelists, psychologists, anthropologists, and mythologists. His body of work was so bold in its implications that it rippled out from the academy into professional fields, and eventually flowed into the public domain via a series of books, films, and a popular series broadcast by public television (the interviews with Bill Moyers). Joe's encyclopedic grasps of mythology, anthropology, literature, philosophy, history, science, psychology, religion, and art were unrivaled in the twentieth century.

In his later years, Joe became a kind of new age celebrity, combining intellectual zeal with charisma and flawless oratory. About Joe, filmmaker and producer George Lucas said,

> It's possible that if I had not run across him I would still be writing Star Wars today. I think you can say about some authors that their work is more important than them. But with Joe, as great as his works are, there is no doubt in my mind that the body of his work is not as great as the man. He is a really wonderful man and he has become my Yoda (Campbell and Cousineau, 1990, 180).

The Meaning of Life

Joe considered trying to find the meaning of life a kind of mental masturbation. It made little sense to him to try to dissect and deconstruct the incomprehensible. But, he was very interested in finding ways to uncover the joy in living.

Rather than reduce life's journey to uncovering a series of concrete answers, Joe embraced its wonder and mystery. There is no excuse for trudging through life listlessly, fearful of taking control of your life. Those who do not follow their bliss live in a world governed by inertia rather than a world of their own creation. In finding a profession, you should find a position which appeals to your heart rather than your bank account.

> There are two approaches to choosing a profession. One is to study the statistics on the number of jobs that are going to be available in this or that category in the next ten years and base your life on that. That's following the rim of the wheel. The other is to ask yourself, "What do I want to do?" If you do that then you are up against your decision. But if you say, "I am going to do what I want to do," and if you stay with it, then something will happen. You may not have a job, but you will have a life, and it will be interesting (Campbell and Osbon, 1991, 266).

You see, when you decide to pursue your passion, all those gnawing, constant worries about practicality and security vanish. If you trust your heart, the details will work themselves out—you will manage to find a place to live, you will have food to eat, and you will manage to survive. Most importantly, you will still be in possession of your soul.

Destiny

For Joe, if a man or woman follows his/her bliss, then they are in sync with Nature and the universe will "line up" accordingly. A person who does not follow his/her bliss lives an artificial life, out of sync with Nature.

> Full circle from the tomb of the womb to the womb of the tomb, we come: an ambiguous enigmatical incursion into a world of solid matter that is soon to melt from us, like the substance of a dream. And, looking back at what had promised to be our own unique,

predictable, and dangerous adventure, all we find in the end is
such a series of standard metamorphoses as men and women have
undergone in every quarter of the world, in all recorded centuries,
and under every odd disguise of civilization (Campbell, 1949, 30).

If you follow your bliss, you put yourself on a track that has been
there all the while just outside of your consciousness. This life you should be
living is waiting for you to seize it. If you seize it, you will have an interesting, fulfilling life. However, you should not confuse "interesting life" with
"predictable and uneventful life." Unless you decide to never set foot outside your door again, you will inevitably encounter some problems along the
way. But, fighting for what you believe in can be an affirmation which
"heightens your experience of being alive" (Campbell and Cousineau, 1990, 20).

If you are on your path, then you have found the place where you can
be transcendent to momentary ups and downs. Nietzsche called this kind of
thinking "love of your fate." Once you are upon the path, whatever your fate,
whatever the hell happens, you say, "This is what I need."

It may look like a wreck, but go at it as though it were an opportunity, a challenge. If you bring love to that moment—not discour-
agement—you will find the strength is there. Any disaster you can
survive is an improvement in your character, your stature, and your
life. What a privilege! This is when the spontaneity of your own
nature will have a chance to flow (Campbell and Osbon, 1991, 38).

As the Buddha observed, by its nature, life involves struggle and
pain. Yet, one can maintain a personal peace, joy, and sense of optimism while
confronting and dealing with life's challenges. If we stay on the path and trust
our hunches, the universe will eventually show us the way.

For when a heart insists on its destiny, resisting the general bland-
ishment, then the agony is great; so too the danger. Forces, however, will have been set in motion beyond the reckoning of the senses. Sequences of events from the corners of the world will draw
gradually together, and miracles of coincidence bring the inevitable
to pass (Campbell and Osbon, 1991, 37).

If you spend a lifetime following your bliss, then when you look back
on your life, you will have few regrets. Your life will seem to be a plot out of
a novel, where seemingly insignificant meetings and coincidences turn out to
be defining moments and, at the end of the story, you understand how all the
pieces fit together. Joe believes that destiny is simply fulfilling the urges that
run deep in your soul. If you devote your life to climbing the ladder of success, you want to be sure that it is against the right wall.

Many of us suppose that our destiny may involve changing the world somehow, making it a better place. While such instincts may be bred of noble intention, altering the universe is beyond the work of mere mortals. However, we have some degree of control over our small part in the world.

To live fully, you must accept the world as it is—replete with its warts, disappointments, and moments of pure joy. The truth about Nature is that life lives on life. When you stop and eat a hamburger at a fast food restaurant, you are eating something that was recently alive. Becoming a vegetarian does not exclude you from the process, either. "Vegetarians are just eating something that can't run away" (Campbell and Osbon, 1991, 119). If you are alive, you are part of the process.

The world will go on long after you have turned to dust. You cannot change much about your mortality nor can you change the laws of Nature. But, you can pursue your bliss and fulfill your destiny, thereby participating fully in the glories and sorrows of the world.

God and Morality

So, half the people in the world are religious people who think that their metaphors are facts. Those are what we call theists. The other half are people who know that the metaphors are not facts and so they're lies. Those are the atheists (Campbell and Cousineau 1990, 136).

The barometer for measuring the viability of a religion should always be its level of compassion. The problem with some religions is that they value narrow interpretations of "sacred texts" over empathy and love. For Joe, if a religion gets you in touch with your bliss and awakens you to the unity of humanity, then it is of value. If not, your religious beliefs are bogus. Joe always said that when you choose your religion, you choose the way in which you will view the world. He liked to tell the story of what a native in the jungle once told a missionary: "Your god keeps himself shut up in a house as if he were old and infirm. Ours is in the forest and in the fields and on the mountains when the rain comes" (Campbell and Flowers, 1991, 21).

Joe dislikes the focus on the negative in the Christian religion—in particular the belief in original sin, and that human beings fall woefully short of the glory of God. The crucifixion is emphasized over the resurrection—the pain and the suffering rather than the final realization and joy.

What has always been basic to Easter or resurrection is crucifixion. If you want resurrection you must have crucifixion. Too many

interpretations of the crucifixion have failed to emphasize that relationship and emphasize instead the calamity of the event. If you
emphasize the calamity you look for someone to blame, which is
why people have blamed the Jews. But, crucifixion is not a calamity if it leads to new life. Through Christ's crucifixion we were
unshelled, which enabled us to be born to resurrection. That is not
a calamity. So, we must take a new look at this event if its symbol-
ism is to be sensed (Campbell and Osbon, 1991, 169).

Whereas the traditional Christian interpretation is one of debt and
repayment, Buddhists see redemption as a process of psychological transformation.

Paul was preaching to a group of merchants, who understood the
whole mystery in terms of economics: there is a debt and you get
an equivalent payment. The debt is enormous, so the payment has
to be enormous. This is all bankers' thinking. Christianity is caught
up in that (Campbell and Osbon, 1991, 145).

In the Garden of Eden, Nature is corrupt. If you believe that Nature
can be evil and arbitrary, then you view Nature as something to be subdued
and feared. Human instincts become impulses that need to be controlled.
However, if Nature is seen as a manifestation of God, then spontaneous
thoughts and actions would be expressions of the divinity—things not to be
suppressed, but celebrated. If your religious beliefs dictate that you are a sin-
ner and you buy into it, then you view life accordingly. Joe thought it would
be much more useful to say, "Bless me, Father, for I have been great. These
are the good things I have done this week."

In several of Joe's books he has pointed out how early Christianity
had a strong mystical tradition influenced by Buddhism. Most of these ten-
dencies were condemned and suppressed as heretical by the early church after
the Council of Nicea in 325. Joe particularly admires the Gospel of Thomas,
dug up in the Egyptian desert in 1948. Like the other four Gospels of the
Bible (Matthew, Mark, Luke and John), the book of Thomas purports to contain the words that Jesus spoke. But, the message in the Gospel of Thomas has
a very different emphasis. Instead of Paradise being an ethereal place visited
after death, the Jesus of the Thomas Gospel contends that Paradise is a choice
in the here and the now, available to every person at every moment. In the
Gospel of Thomas, Jesus resides in all of us and is present everywhere at all
times:

Whoever drinks from my mouth shall become as I am and I myself
will become he, and the hidden things shall be revealed to him. . .

I am the All, the All came forth from me and the All attained to me.
Cleave a piece of wood, I am there; lift up the stone and you will
find me there (Peuch, 1984, 28-30).

According to the Gospel of Thomas, The Kingdom is spread upon the
earth now. It is just that most humans do not see it. If Paradise is living in the
world as it is, then eternity ceases to have as much power as a threat or even-
tual reward.

> Eternity has nothing to do with time. Eternity is that dimension of
> here and now that all thinking in temporal terms cuts off. And if
> you don't get it here, you won't get it anywhere. The problem with
> heaven is that you will be having such a good time there, you won't
> even think of eternity. You'll just have this unending delight in the
> beatific vision of God. But the experience of eternity right here and
> now, in all things, whether thought of as good or as evil, is the func-
> tion of life (Campbell and Flowers, 1991, 67).

Money

Joe's parents were not rich, but his father made enough in his manu-
facturing business to take the family on trips abroad whenever the bank
account was flush. As a young man, Joe lived through the stock market crash
of 1929 and the Great Depression, so he saw firsthand how poverty can over-
take even the proudest of families. In his mid-twenties, he still had not found
a real, full-time job, but he was in no rush for one. He found that he didn't
need much money, and at the time, he had more pressing things to do, such as
reading books, traveling, and playing the saxophone.

But, it is folly to ignore the power of money in a capitalistic society.
The more money you possess, the greater your life possibilities. Despite
money's allure, it has a downside—you can forget about your life in the fren-
zy to attain it. People who live and work for money can turn themselves into
slaves, doing work they hate. If you follow your bliss, you spend your time
doing what you love to do, so getting paid for it is a bonus.

> Work begins when you don't like what you're doing. There's a wise
> saying: make your hobby your source of income. Then there's no
> such thing as work, and there's no such thing as getting tired. That's
> been my own experience. I did just what I wanted to do. It takes a
> little courage at first, because they've all got a lot of plans for you.
> But you can make it happen (Campbell et al., 1990, 107).

If you follow your bliss, then you will love your work and would do
it, even if you were never going to earn a dollar from it. However, when you

work out of love, then money will come to you because you will be giving life and "life responds in the way of its counterpart in hard coin" (Campbell and Osbon, 1991, 58).

When the Road is Smooth

Nothing can happen to you which is not positive (Campbell and Osbon, 1991, 39).

When the road is smooth, it probably means that you are on the right track. But, it is not important whether the road is smooth or rocky. If you have decided to chart your own path, then the momentary thrill of a smooth ride or the unsettling jolt of potholes are irrelevant. What is important is to continue on the quest. Your quest.

When the Road Gets Rocky

When asked how to respond to life's problems, Joe was fond of quoting the *Koran*, "Do you think that you shall enter the Garden of Bliss without such trials as came to those who passed away before you?" In other words, challenges are simply a part of life. If you succumb to external forces and allow others to dissuade you on your quest, then you are not following your bliss. Rather, you are choosing to live "a wasteland existence" and live at the whim of others.

Once, in the latter part of his life, Joe was asked to serve on a panel to discuss mythology and religion in a public forum. During the session, a fellow member of the panel would attack Joe and his work on every possible point. While it is not uncommon in academia to have vociferous arguments, this fellow's invectives were often personal and most inappropriate. Joe, with his elegant manners, was quite taken aback. After a short break, a member of the audience asked Joe why he did not respond to the personal and professional accusations of his colleague. Nonplussed, Joe said, "As you walk down the path of life, birds will shit on you. Do not bother to stop and brush it off" (Campbell and Osbon, 1991, 20). The audience erupted in spontaneous, thundering applause.

When You Encounter a Dragon in the Middle of the Road

Campbell would advise you to learn to live with the dragon and to discover ways to derive joy from the relationship. "The first step is in the recognition of the monstrous nature of life and its glory in that character: the realization that this is just how it is and that it cannot and will not be changed. So if you really want to help this world, what you will have to teach is how to live in it." (Campbell, 1972, 106).

The Crux

1. Find a special place where you can be alone to meditate about your life. Make this special place uniquely your own—no one else's. Regularly return to refresh yourself. This is your kingdom in miniature, where you create the life worth living.
2. Read all the books that speak to your heart. Always keep thinking, reading, and growing.
3. Discover who you are. Spend your time doing what you love.
4. Never do anything solely for money. If you take money for something you don't believe in, you pay with your soul.
5. Once you find your bliss, follow it with all your might. Have courage, be bold.
6. Although people have different backgrounds, cultures, and religions, we are unified by our desires, dreams, and frailties. The universe is one cell and we all share responsibility for its welfare. Have compassion. Love thy neighbor.
7. If you follow your bliss, the universe will open up for you. However, this does not mean that your path will always be smooth.
8. Life is full of ecstasy and tragedy, perfect just the way it is. You cannot rid the world of sorrows and you can't alter Nature. However, you have the power to change your life, to create the life you want.
9. If you feel frustrated and depressed about your life, do something about it. Change it. Do not wait around for someone else to save you. Only you can save yourself.
10. Lead an extraordinary life. Accept nothing less.

In a Nutshell

If you have the guts to follow the risk, however, life opens, opens, and opens up all along the line. I'm not superstitious, but I do believe in spiritual magic, you might say. I feel that if one follows what I call one's "bliss"—the thing that really gets you deep in the gut and that you feel is your life—doors will open up. They do! They have in my life and they have in many lives I know of (Campbell et al., 1990, 57).

The Wisdom of Joseph Campbell

On Change

When skies get dull with no prospect of clearing, run away, change your home town—your name—your job—change anything. No misfortune can be worse than the misfortune of resting permanently static. Take a chance—if you lose you are scarcely worse-off than before—if you win you have at least experience and a new thrill or two gained (Larsen and Larsen, 1991, 66).

On Poetry

Poets are simply those who have made a profession and a lifestyle of being in touch with their bliss (Campbell and Flowers, 1991, 118).

On Writing

Writer's block results from too much head. Cut off your head. Pegasus, poetry, was born of Medusa when her head was cut off. You have to be reckless when writing. Be as crazy as your conscience allows (Campbell et al., 1990, 270).

On Sports

When I was running at Columbia, I ran a couple of races that were just beautiful. During the second race, I knew I was going to win even though there was no reason for me to know this, because I was touched off as anchor in the relay with the leading runner thirty yards ahead of me. But I just knew, and it was my peak experience. Nobody could beat me that day. That's being in full form and really knowing it. I don't think I have ever done anything in my life as competently as I ran those two races—it was the experience of really being at my full and doing a perfect job (Campbell and Flowers, 1991, 220).

On Money

Money experienced as life energy is indeed a meditation, and letting it flow out instead of hoarding it is a mode of participation in the lives of others (Campbell et al., 1990, 59).

On Marriage

You see, the whole thing in marriage is the relationship and yielding—knowing the functions, knowing that each is playing a role in an organism. One of the things I have realized—and people who have been married a long time realize—is that marriage is not a love affair. A love affair has to do with immediate personal satisfaction. But marriage is an ordeal; it means yielding, time and again. That's why it's a sacrament: you give up your personal simplicity to participate in a relationship. And when you're giving, you're not giving to the other person: you're giving to the relationship. And if you realize that you are in the relationship just as the other person is, then it becomes life building, a life-fostering and enriching experience, not an impoverishment because you're giving to somebody else...What a beautiful thing is a life together as growing personalities, each helping the other to flower, rather than just moving into the standard archetype. It's a wonderful moment when people can make the decision to be something quite astonishing and unexpected, rather than cookie-mold products (Campbell et al., 1990, 127).

On Aging

Aging is really like having this old car. The fender gets dented, a headlight's knocked out, the bumper falls off, and you just have to let them go (Larsen and Larsen, 1991, 552).

On Old Age

One great thing about growing old is that nothing is going to lead to anything. Everything is of the moment (Campbell and Osbon, 1991, 20).

On Ideals

Ideals are dangerous. Don't take them seriously. You can get by on a few (Campbell and Osbon, 1991, 134-135).

Joseph Campbell's Daily Goals

(From his journals when he was in his twenties, Larsen and Larsen, 1991, 144)
1. at least the minimum physical exercise per day
2. at least three long walks per week
3. at least two sunbaths (1.5 hours each) per week
4. four hours fiction writing per day; produce four short stories by September 26
5. four hours fiction reading per day; modern American lit
6. at least one observation of setting, character, pantomime, speech, per day
7. at least one new light on one of the following phases of remembering: mom, dad, my biography
8. careful diary of my reactions, plans, etc., as an attempt to crystallize, more or less, my essential point of view, or at least discover what that point of view may be
9. listen; question; don't expound

Important Dates

1904	Born in New York City, March 26 to Charles and Josephine Campbell, an upper middle class family
1915	Shows interest in American Indian cultures, impressed with the collection of totem poles in the American Museum of Natural History in New York
1919	Attends Canterbury Preparatory School in New Milford
1922	Transfers from Dartmouth College to Columbia, where he decides to run track; parents continue to "keep to the program" of world travel for the family
1927	Receives M.A. in English and comparative literature at Columbia University
1927	Goes to Europe for postgraduate study in Arthurian romances at University of Munich and University of Paris
1929	Returns to the United States, where he lives the simple life— reading books and playing jazz in Woodstock, New York. For a year, he heads out to Carmel, California, where he hangs out with Ed Ricketts and John Steinbeck. Campbell falls in love with Steinbeck's wife, Carol. Eventually, he makes his

1934	way back to New York.
1934	Begins teaching at Sarah Lawrence College
1938	Marries a graduate student, Jean Erdman, who later becomes a star in Martha Graham's dance company
1949	*Hero with a Thousand Faces* published
1952	Edits *The Portable Arabian Nights*
1959-1968	*Masks of God* published (Primitive Mythology, 1959; Oriental Mythology, 1962; Occidental Mythology, 1964; Creative Mythology, 1968)
1971	Edits *The Portable Jung*
1984	*The Inner Reaches* of Outer Space published
1985-1986	*The Power of Myth* filmed at George Lucas' ranch
1987	Dies at age 83 in Honolulu, Hawaii, October 31

References and Resources

Campbell, J. 1949. *The Hero With a Thousand Faces*. Princeton, NJ: Princeton University Press.

Campbell, J. 1972. *Masks of God, Volumes 1-4*. New York: Viking.

Campbell, J. 1972. *Myths to Live By*. New York: Viking.

Campbell, J. & Osbon, D. ed. 1991. *A Joseph Campbell Companion*. New York: HarperCollins.

Campbell, J., & Flowers, B. ed. with Moyers, B. 1991. *The Power of Myth*. New York: Bantam Doubleday

Campbell, J., Toms, M., & Maher, J. ed. & Biggs, D. 1990. *An Open Life: Joseph Campbell in Conversation with Michael Toms*. New York: HarperCollins.

Campbell, J., & Cousineau, P. ed. 1990. The Hero's Journey: *The World of Joseph Campbell*. New York: HarperCollins.

Campbell, J., & Kennedy, E. ed. 2001. Thou Art That: Transforming Religious Metaphor. Novato, CA: New World Library.

Larsen, S., & Larsen, R. 1991. *A Fire in the Mind: The Life of Joseph Campbell*. New York: Doubleday.

Peuch, H. 1984. *The Gospel According to Thomas*. San Francisco: HarperCollins.

NOTES

Courtesy of The Wilson House

BILL WILSON

(1895-1971)

Anonymous

In May, 1935, a failed stockbroker from New York City named Bill Wilson met a proctologist named Dr. Bob Smith in Akron, Ohio. Their chance meeting—perhaps an act of Providence—has saved the lives of millions of alcoholics. Jointly, they formed an organization that has helped men and women around the world regain control over their lives. Although his name may not be familiar to the general public, every recovering alcoholic in AA knows the name Bill Wilson. He wrote the book <u>Alcoholics Anonymous</u> (1939), the namesake of the AA program, and was the voice of AA until his death in 1971 at age seventy-six.

> Believe more deeply. Hold your face up to the Light, even though
> for the moment you do not see (from a letter, 1950).

Presumptuous indeed, for one alcoholic to write of the life and beliefs of Bill Wilson. You see, every recovering alcoholic in Alcoholics Anonymous owes his/her life to Bill Wilson. In this strange and utterly democratic fellowship we find sobriety, and for the alcoholic sobriety is life. In AA, we also rediscover what it means to be alive. We are no dour and grim bunch of white-knuckle drunks desperately trying to get through another 24 hours without picking up a drink. We are generally a happy bunch. Laughter punctuates all of our meetings; we enjoy the camaraderie of survivors in a pretty tough school. No matter our backgrounds or present circumstances, we are all people who have come back from the edge of the abyss. So we owe Bill our lives in a physical sense—because to drink is to die. And also in the spiritual sense—in AA we found a Life we never thought possible.

In 1933, Bill Wilson was admitted to the alcoholic ward of the Towns Hospital in New York City for the first time. Dr. William Silkworth, who treated him there, knew that like other chronic alcoholics Wilson was likely doomed to a future of insanity or death. From a promising start as a businessman on Wall Street after he served in the Army in World War I, he was reduced to being supported by his wife Lois and living with his father-in-law. He would be in and out of the Towns Hospital three times in the next year. However, before entering Towns Hospital for a fourth time in December 1934, he met an old drinking buddy (a man named Ebby) who had found help through a Christian organization known as the Oxford Group. The meeting profoundly affected Wilson. Never a religious man, Bill had a vision while at the hospital and emerged from the experience with the conviction that he must live by certain ethical principles and that he should dedicate himself to helping other drunks.

Wilson sought out the help of the proctologist, Dr. Bob Smith, and they attempted to come up with a plan. After several spectacular failures, they eventually started the first AA group in Akron, Ohio (the Kings School Group, which still meets). By 1937, Bill and Dr. Bob counted heads, and 40 drunks were staying sober in Akron, New York, and Cleveland. They knew they had stumbled onto something, and Bill convinced the Akron group that a book needed to be written to share their stories and program of recovery with other alcoholics. Bill started the *Big Book* in 1938. By the time it was published the following year, there were 100 sober alcoholics in the fellowship. AA members are noted for their outspoken opinions anyway, so managing to create a book that would please all of the constituents must have been quite a challenge. What it taught Bill about patience, we don't know, but it surely taught him a lot about endurance.

The *Big Book*, by the way, earned its name because the first printing of the first edition literally was big. They printed it on cheap, thick paper, and it was quite a handful. The book cost $3.50 in 1939, quite expensive for the time, and Wilson wanted readers to think they got their monies worth. Although AA does not keep rolls of members, there are an estimated three million of us in 146 countries. The *Big Book* has been translated into 40 languages.

Bill's writing in *Alcoholics Anonymous* is in the first section that outlines the program of recovery in AA. That section also contains his personal story. The bulk of the book is taken up with the personal stories of recovery by members of the fellowship. The book is now in its third edition, and although some of the Old Timers' stories remain, the first 164 pages in which Wilson outlines the program of recovery have never been changed. A fourth edition is being prepared, but the first section will certainly remain intact. Bill was not done writing when the *Big Book* was published. He wrote four other books (still used at AA meetings) and contributed heavily to two others. He wrote hundreds of articles for AA's magazine, *The Grapevine*, and untold thousands of letters to alcoholics around the world. Four principles—hope, faith, humility, service—characterize the life of Bill Wilson and find resonance in the lives of non-alcoholics, as well as those of us in recovery.

Hope

Hope may be the most precious of human emotions. Perhaps only love, in all of its myriad forms, is more important. But in moments when we are at the end of our resources, it is hope that sustains us. Hope can be fleeting, but it is also a gift that we can give to others. There is no more beautiful expression of the hope suffering alcoholics find in AA than this description Bill wrote into his discussion of the 12-steps (the guiding commandments of AA).

> If we are painstaking about this phase of our development, we will be amazed before we are halfway through. We are going to know a new freedom and a new happiness. We will not regret the past nor wish to shut the door on it. We will comprehend the word serenity and we will know peace. No matter how far down the scale we have gone, we will see how our experience can benefit others. That feeling of uselessness and self-pity will disappear. We will lose interest in selfish things and gain interest in our fellows. Self-seeking will slip away. Our whole attitude and outlook upon life will change. Fear of people and of economic insecurity will leave us. We will intuitively know how to handle situations that used to baffle us. We will suddenly realize that God is doing for us what we could not do for ourselves. Are these extravagant promises? We think not. They are being fulfilled among us—sometimes quickly, sometimes slowly. They will always materialize if we work for them ("Alcoholics Anonymous" 1939, 53-54).

Hope for a better life is what every man and woman finds at the first meeting. In many ways, Bill Wilson gave hope to the hopeless.

Faith

Faith is the cornerstone of the AA way of life. Bill himself was a skeptic until his meeting with a friend (Ebby), who found sobriety in religion. But when Bill admitted himself to the Towns Hospital for the last time, in 1934, it was there that he had the vision that he describes in this way.

> My depression deepened unbearably and finally it seemed to me as though I were at the very bottom of the pit. I still gagged badly on the notion of a Power greater than myself, but finally, just for the moment, the last vestige of my proud obstinacy was crushed. All at once, I found myself crying out, 'If there is a God, let Him show Himself! I am ready to do anything, anything!' Suddenly the room lit up with a great white light. I was caught up into an ecstasy which there is no word to describe. It seemed to me, in the mind's eye, that I was on a mountain and that a wind not of air but of spirit was blowing. And then it burst upon me that I was a free man ("AA Comes of Age" 1957, 63).

Bill said later that he never again doubted the existence of God. However, after vainly trying to urge drunks to have the same ecstatic experience he had, he came to understand that there are other ways to come to spiritual awareness. Out of his earlier skepticism and his experience with a religious revival movement known as the Oxford Groups (the group who had rescued his friend Ebby), and his meeting with Dr. Bob there grew the broad inclusiveness that is found in the 12 steps. Bill Wilson's gift of faith to the fellowship of Alcoholics Anonymous is a faith that is accessible to the most hardened and streetwise alcoholic—if he is willing to accept the steps of the program of AA.

> We have found that God does not make too hard terms with those who seek Him. To us, the realm of the spirit is broad, roomy, all inclusive, never exclusive or forbidding to those who earnestly seek. It is open, we believe, to all ("Alcoholics Anonymous" 1939, 46).

By that simple expediency, AA became accessible to the non-religious, as well as to men and woman of all faiths.

Humility

When we first stumble in the doors of AA meeting rooms, we think the anonymity of the program is to protect us from being found out. And that is real enough. But gradually, we come to feel that the Anonymous in our name has another meaning—not taking credit publicly for the gift God has given us, nor for the work we do in AA. Public recognition is simply not in the spirit of AA.

With regard to humility, Bill's life was a fine example. None of the books he wrote bear his name except the title of *As Bill Sees It*, and then only his first name both in the title and the introduction written to AA members. In 1954, Yale University offered him an honorary Doctor of Laws degree in recognition of his work with alcoholics. After some soul searching, he gracefully declined. He also turned down *Time* magazine's offer to put him on their cover, even though the editors suggested they photograph the back of his head. He declined the cover story as well, admitting that "it wasn't easy" ("Pass It On" 1984, 314). His wife Lois said that "Bill felt very strongly that of all things he should not set himself up as superior in any way to other alcoholics. … He was a tremendous egoist. But he recognized this, and I believe that the triumph of his life was his victory over himself and his becoming truly humble" ("Pass It On" 1984, 313).

Service

> When anyone, anywhere, reaches out for help, I want the hand of AA always to be there. And for that: I am responsible (Declaration of the 30th International Convention of Alcoholics Anonymous 1965).

Once we find freedom from the compulsion to drink by working the 12 steps of AA, we find happiness in service to others. Our twelfth step prescribes it, and AA members are legendary for untiringly giving themselves to help drunks. Alcoholics Anonymous really began because Bill was convinced that he had to help another suffering alcoholic if he were to keep sober himself. AA's legacy of service is all the more remarkable because it is done anonymously, without fanfare, in back alleys, back rooms, drunk wards, jails, asylums, bars, in housing projects and in homes of the socially prominent.

When Bill Wilson sobered up he was 39 years old. Half of his life lay before him, and he gave it all in service to AA. Bill never had another steady job other than shepherding first the groups and then the service office of Alcoholics Anonymous.

In many places and in many ways, Bill said essentially what he wrote in the AA Service Manual (1962), "We must carry the message, else we ourselves can wither and those who haven't been given the truth may die" (5). Carry the message he did, the rest of his life.

When the Road Is Smooth

Many people wonder how AA can function under a seeming anarchy. Other societies have to have law and force and sanction and punishment, administered by authorized people. Happily for us, we found that we need no human authority whatever. We have two authorities which are far more effective. One is benign, the other malign. There is God, our Father, who very simply says, "I am waiting for you to do my will." The other authority is named John Barleycorn, and he says, "You had better do God's will or I will kill you" ("As Bill Sees It" 1967, 319).

When the Road Gets Rocky

God grant us the serenity to accept the things we cannot change, courage to change the things we can, and wisdom to know the difference. Widely known as the *Serenity Prayer*, it came to the AA fellowship from an obituary in a New York City newspaper. It was written by Reinhold Niebuhr.

When You Encounter a Dragon in the Middle of the Road

Don't drink. Call your sponsor. Go to meetings (AA slogan). For Bill Wilson and other recovering alcoholics, the Dragon is always alcohol and the urge to drink. To drink is to suffer and die.

The Crux: Bill Wilson's Advice for Getting a Life

Wilson's lasting legacy to mankind is found on two pages that open Chapter 5 in the *Big Book*—pages 59 and 60. There he wrote the twelve steps of Alcoholics Anonymous, which are explained in terms of practical living and illustrated in the stories of recovering alcoholics.

The 12 Steps of Alcoholics Anonymous

1. We admitted we were powerless over alcohol—that our lives had become unmanageable.
2. Came to believe that a Power greater than ourselves could restore us to sanity.
3. Made a decision to turn our will and our lives over to the care of God *as we understood Him.*
4. Made a searching and fearless moral inventory of ourselves.
5. Admitted to God, to ourselves, and to another human being the exact nature of our wrongs.
6. Were entirely ready to have God remove all these defects of character.
7. Humbly asked Him to remove our shortcomings.
8. Made a list of all persons we had harmed, and became willing to make amends to them all.
9. Made direct amends to such people wherever possible, except when to do so would injure them or others.
10. Continued to take personal inventory and when we were wrong, promptly admitted it.
11. Sought through prayer and meditation to improve our conscious contact with God *as we understood Him*, praying only for knowledge of His will for us and the power to carry that out.
12. Having had a spiritual awakening as the result of these steps, we tried to carry this message to alcoholics and to practice these principles in all our affairs.

These are the stepping stones to recovery, familiar to members of AA, the legacy of Bill Wilson. Since 1939, the twelve steps have been shared freely with other organizations, such as Narcotics Anonymous. Alcoholic or not, the 12-steps provide a plan for living that could work well for anyone.

In a Nutshell

Such is the paradox of AA regeneration: strength arising out of complete defeat and weakness, the loss of one's old life as a condition for finding a new one ("As Bill Sees It" 1967, 49).

Trust God. Clean house. Help others (AA slogan).

The Wisdom of Bill Wilson

On Ambition

True ambition is not what we thought it was. True ambition is to walk humbly under the grace of God (from the *Big Book*).

On Defeat

We perceive that only through utter defeat we are able to take our first steps towards liberation and strength. Our admissions of personal powerlessness finally turn out to be a firm bedrock upon which happy and purposeful lives may be built. (from the *Big Book*)

On Dependency

The real current can't flow until our paralyzing dependencies are broken, and broken at depth. Only then can we possibly have a glimmer of what adult love really is (from *Emotional Sobriety*).

On Destiny

We are going to know a new freedom and a new happiness. We will not regret the past nor wish to shut the door on it. We will comprehend the word serenity and we will know peace. No matter how far down the scale we have gone, we will see how our experience can benefit others. That feeling of uselessness and self-pity will disappear. We will lose interest in selfish things and gain interest in our fellows. Self-seeking will slip away. Our whole attitude and outlook upon life will change. Fear of people and of economic insecurity will leave us. We will intuitively know how to handle situations which used to baffle us. We will suddenly realize that God is doing for us what we could not do ourselves (from the *Big Book*).

On Resentment

It is plain that a life which includes deep resentment leads only to futility and unhappiness. To the precise extent that we permit these...we squander the hours that might have been worth while (from the *Big Book*).

On Being a Victim

Plainly, I could not avail myself of God's love until I was able to offer it back to Him by loving others as He would have me. And I couldn't possibly do that so long as I was victimized by false dependencies (from *Emotional Sobriety*).

On Faith

All men of faith have courage. They trust their God. We never apologize for God. Instead we let Him demonstrate, through us, what He can do. We ask Him to remove our fear and direct our attention to what He would have us be. At once, we commence to outgrow fear (from the *Big Book*).

Important Dates

1895	November 26, Bill Wilson is born in East Dorset, Vermont
1917	World War I, Bill joins the Army
1918	Bill marries Lois Burnham
1925-1933	Bill works as stock broker. At first successful, his drinking and the stock market crash ruin him.
1933	Bill is committed to Towns Hospital for the first time
1934	Bill's last drink. Bill's spiritual experience in the Towns Hospital.
1935	In May, Bill and Dr. Bob meet; June 10, Dr. Bob's last drink (Alcoholics Anonymous dates its beginning from this day)
1937	More than 40 alcoholics are staying sober; the *Big Book*, *Alcoholics Anonymous*, is begun
1939	*Alcoholics Anonymous* is published
1941	Jack Alexander's article in the *Saturday Evening Post* makes AA nationally known; AA membership increases dramatically
1950	First International AA Convention; Dr. Bob dies, November 16
1955	Bill formally turns the governance of AA over to the groups at the St. Louis Convention

1971   Bill Wilson dies, January 24

References and Resources

AA Service Manual. 1962. New York: AA World Services, Inc.
Alcoholics Anonymous. 1939, 1955, 1976. New York: AA World Services, Inc.
Alcoholics Anonymous Comes of Age: A Brief History of AA. 1957. New York: AA World Services, Inc.
As Bill Sees It (The AA Way of Life). 1967. New York: AA World Services, Inc.
Pass It On: Bill Wilson and How the AA Message Reached the World. 1984. New York: AA World Services, Inc.

NOTES

Courtesy of Alan Storey

GERDA WEISSMANN KLEIN
(1924-)

By Hal Foster

Gerda Weissmann Klein has written a moving memoir (<u>All But My Life</u>) about the resiliency of the human spirit, spoken all over the world, appeared on numerous television shows, and has had a film made of her life which won both an Emmy and an Oscar. She also serves as head of the Gerda and Kurt Klein Foundation, an organization whose mission is to teach toler-ance and to conquer hunger. In addition, Gerda is an official spokesperson for Columbine High School. Not bad for a 78-year-old woman with a tenth grade education.

When she accepted the award for the Oscar for the film based upon her life at the Academy Awards, Gerda gave the only memorable speech of that April night in 1996. The moment captures Gerda's personality in many ways—her eloquence as a speaker, her authenticity and selflessness, her relentless determination to further the cause of human compassion. Gerda was also awarded the Emmy, and two Cable Ace Awards.

I have learned that we must occasionally pause on that steep climb to whatever summit we are seeking, take a backward glance, and be grateful for how far we have come. I have found that for me the

meaning of life was not gained at a summit, whatever the achievement might be. Summits tend to be windy, cold, and lonely. Nor
have I found the answer to the meaning of life in the abyss of
hunger, abuse, and pain. The crest of my dreams during the years
of slavery in the camps were thoughts of an evening at home with
my family (Klein & Klein, 2000, 274-275).

Gerda Weissmann was born in Bielsko, Poland, on May 8, 1924. She
adored her older brother Artur and grew up with loving parents and good
friends in a happy middle class home. However, in 1939 when the Nazis
invaded Poland, everything changed. Suddenly, the family was ordered to live
in their cold, damp basement without water or electrity. After two months in
the basement, the Nazis ordered her brother Artur to a labor camp. Three
years later, she and her parents were sent off as well. She would never see any
of her family again. Eventually, she learned that both of her parents had been
killed, but she never discovered what happened to her brother Artur.

One reason Gerda was not killed immediately was because she was
young and could be used as a worker in a camp. At age 18, she was sent to
slave labor camps for the next three years of her life (1942-1945). While
being held prisoner at a camp that milled cloth, Gerda was aware of one
humanitarian gesture, even from her captors. One day, Frau Kugler, a super-
visor at the cloth mill in which Gerda worked, accosted her and said, "Pull
yourself together, Gerda, it is a matter of life or death!" As Gerda went back
to work with renewed vigor, she noticed that the mill was being inspected by
a notoriously sadistic SS officer, a man fond of shipping ailing Jews to
Auschwitz for "processing." Gerda (1957) writes:

"Thank you," I whispered.
"It's all right." She touched my hand. "Who knows—?" She broke
it off there, and as she went out of the door I looked after her in
wonder. The German woman who worked for the SS had saved my
life (133).

As the Allied victory became imminent the Germans evacuated the
labor camp at Gruenberg, site of Gerda's camp. The Germans forced 2000
young girls to march during the coldest part of winter for 350 miles. Of the
2000 only about 120 survived the march. At the end of the march, the
Germans forced the surviving girls into a vacant factory. The Germans placed
a time bomb detonated to explode in the factory with the girls. Because of
torrential rains, the bomb never went off.

The U.S. Fifth Infantry Division rescued the remaining prisoners on May 6, 1945. Among the rescuers was a young Jewish lieutenant, Kurt Klein. One year later, Gerda and Kurt married in Paris. Soon, the couple moved to Buffalo, New York, where Kurt established a printing business. It was in Buffalo that Gerda began work on her remarkable memoir, *All But My Life*.

Except for Kurt, Gerda knew no one in the United States. She began writing *All But My Life* in German, but found it intolerable to write in the language of her tormentors. She resumed writing the book in English, even though English was a relatively new language to Gerda.

> The knowledge that my native tongue became repugnant to me strengthened my resolve to steep myself even more in my new language. It was fascinating to choose words from this seemingly inexhaustible font. I would acquire them in order to express what I needed to say (Klein, 1957, 256).

She began learning English by reading the labels of food products in supermarkets. To supplement her self instruction, Gerda decided to audit a writing course at the University of Buffalo. By coincidence, her instructor for the course was Sloan Wilson, author of *The Man in the Gray Flannel Suit*. Sloan Wilson asked to see her work. After reading a draft of *All But My Life*, Wilson told the aspiring writer, "There is nothing I can teach you, but I would like to help you get it published." Eventually, Arthur Wang, of Hill and Wang (now Farrar, Straus and Giroux) decided to take a chance on *All But My Life*, "even if it doesn't earn a penny." It turned out that *All But My Life* was an extremely successful book (now in its 51st edition).

Love and Family

If you have ever heard her speak or read any of her writings, you know that faith and family provide the center for Gerda Weissmann Klein's life. During her imprisonment, it was remembrances of family that kept her alive during the bleakest hours.

> And as always when in despair, I started to think of my homecoming. I placed and replaced details upon details, playing with the fragments of my dreams. Who would come home first? I always wished that I should come last—walk into the house to find them all there. At times, I thought I would reach home late at night. The house would be dark. I would not wake them (Klein, 1957, 177).

Upon two occasions, her father saved her life. Once, during the initial terrifying stages of the Nazi takeover, Gerda sank into a deep depression and even considered ending her life.

> It seemed almost a luxury to die, to go to sleep and never wake up again. Then I felt Papa's hand on my shoulder. I didn't turn. He put his hand on the nape of my neck and turned me forcibly toward him. He looked steadily at me and then answered my thoughts.
> "Whatever you are thinking now is wrong. It is cowardly."
> I couldn't deny it. He lifted my chin up and looked at me firmly again.
> "Promise me that no matter what happens you will never do it."
> I couldn't speak.
> "I want your promise now."
> "I promise you Papa," and in the years to come, when death seemed the only solution, I remembered that promise as my most sacred vow (Klein, 1957, 32).

The second time her father saved her life was just before the three remaining family members were forced to leave their home and sent to slave camps. Just before her father was taken away, he insisted Gerda put on her ski boots. Gerda abided by her father's wishes. Later, she and two thousand other prisoners were forced to march during the bitterest winter weather and most did not survive the ordeal. Wearing those boots probably kept her alive.

As a prisoner enduring incredible hardship, torture, and near-starvation, Gerda became fearful that she might somehow lose the ability to bear children. In America, she and Kurt eventually had a family of three, and eight grandchildren. Her children and grandchildren are the triumph over the forces of destruction.

> Each time I held one of our newborn children in my arms, the feeling would return that I had been entrusted with a sacred legacy from those in my family who had been deprived of life. Overcome by an awed gratitude, I felt annointed by the privilege of being a conduit, a link between the past and the future (Klein & Klein, 2000, 273-274).

Gerda's love of children has played out in other, unpredictable ways. For example, in the chaotic aftermath of the Columbine High School shootings, Gerda received an invitation to speak. Gerda told students, "Good can and must emerge from tragedy." As a result, students at the school formed an organization called *Heart of Columbine*, dedicated to alleviating hunger. About Gerda, one student said, "She's so strong, it makes us want to help other people" (Rubin, 2002).

74

Never Yield to Evil

During their brutal imprisonment in slave labor camps, Gerda and her young friends showed a strong spirit. On a Yom Kippur, the Jewish day of fasting, the girls who were already on the verge of starvation, were still determined to fast.

> We had been in camp for three months when Yom Kippur, the Day of Atonement, came. We all said that we would fast. Meister Zimmer somehow heard about it. He warned that severe punishment would be meted out to anyone who feigned illness or did not produce the prescribed amount of material. Nevertheless, we all fasted. We worked harder than ever but no one touched food until there were three stars in the evening sky. There was a proud serenity about every one of us, a sense of accomplishment (Klein, 1957, 127).

Even birthdays were celebrated with ingenuity. On one particularly memorable birthday, Gerda remembers how her fellow prisoners managed to make small, homemade mementos from scraps of yarn and spools. One friend even managed to pluck a flower through the barbed wire of the fence from the director's garden to offer as a present. To thank her friends for their generosity one Christmas eve, Gerda wrote and performed a humorous skit, which provided some much needed laughter to the camp. Gerda considers the skit as one of her greatest achievements in life.

Once she arrived in America, Gerda began trying to help the less fortunate, especially children. Even as a newlywed in Buffalo, she began devoting time to the Jewish Federation. The recipient of seven honorary Doctorates of Humane Letters (the last from Chapman University, awarded for the first time to a couple), the recipient of the Human Rights Award (given by the National Lawyers' Committee for Human Rights), and president of a foundation (The Kurt and Gerda Weissmann Foundation) whose focus is to eliminate hatred and hunger, Gerda believes that the welfare of the planet is dependent upon our willingness to help each other.

> The idea of helping others need not be confined to victims of the Holocaust. The welfare of all children has always been of utmost importance to me: the abused, the handicapped, the underprivileged, the ill. I can identify with them because I know what it is like not to be able to communicate one's pain and hope. I had learned,

above all, that even after cataclysmic events I was able to laugh again (250, All But My Life).

When the Road is Smooth

Savor the good times, but always remember the less fortunate and use your strength to help them.

When the Road Gets Rocky

Take the long view. Do not allow temporary setbacks to alter your goals. "Each day begins with a sunrise and will continue to do so long after all our concerns and disappointments have been lost in the sands of time" (Klein, 1957, 275).

The Crux

1. Helping others is helping yourself.
2. Never forget the past but live in the present.
3. Do not take for granted the good days. A boring night at home may some-day be the finest memory you will have. Savor it.

In a Nutshell

All of us have a reservoir of untapped strength that comes to the fore at moments of crisis (Klein, 1957, 250).

The Wisdom of Gerda Weissmann Klein

On Responsibility

As I finish the Last Chapter of my book, I feel at peace, at last. I have discharged a burden, and paid a debt to many nameless heroes, resting in their unmarked graves. For I am haunted by the thought that I might be the only one left to tell their story.

Happy in my new life, I have pened the last sentence of the past. I have written my story with tears and with love, in the hope that my children, safely asleep in their cribs, should not awake from a nightmare and find it to be reality (Klein, 1957, preface).

On Family

Inevitably, we all revert to the core of our existence in moments of crisis and look for our lodestar. I have tried to follow mine ever since I left my parents and my childhood home. I know full well what saw me through those unspeakable years. It was the powerful memory of an evening at home (Klein, 1957, 260).

On Meeting Life's Challenges

"Be strong!" And I heard it again like an echo: "Be strong." Those were my mother's last words to me (Klein, 1957, 92).

On Keeping Your Perspective

There was one Bielskso girl, Greta, whom I liked in particular. She was always cheerful. 'You know,' she said to me one day, 'I actually was never happier than now.' I gasped in sheer disbelief, and then she told me her story. She had been born out of wedlock. Her mother had always worked and Greta had never had a home. She had drifted from family to family. Some children were not allowed to play with her. "I looked at all those kids," she said, "and you were probably among them—with your frilly dresses, your patent leather shoes, your fretting nannies and doting parents. I always was on the outside. Now finally we are equals. Yes it's true, I have never been happier than I am now" (Klein, 1957, 127).

On Helping the Less Fortunate

Every so often I believed that I was coming to some better understanding of my past, that I could begin to handle the memories, that the pain of my losses was diminishing and would no longer intrude on the present, only to find that the scars of my experience would remain for life. I feel renewed pain and anger whenever I see refugees, identify with and recall pangs of hunger on seeing the emaciated faces and bodies of children. That pain is most acute whenever I see a lonely, crying child, even if that child is not otherwise deprived or abused. I know from long experience that specific pain will lessen and ultimately pass, but I have never been able to free myself altogether of those emotions. The truth is that at this stage of my life, removed from the immediate concerns of raising a family or making my way in a profession, I have more time to reflect, and let the wanton suffering inflicted on millions come into sharper focus. The past remains vivid and the inhumanity an enigma (Klein & Klein, 2000, 215-216).

On America

In retrospect, I think that coming to America was like stepping out of a dark, oppressive room in which I had been locked up for a long, long time. Once I was free and exposed to light again, the most ordinary objects, the simplest things acquired an aura of extraordinary beauty, desirability, and value. I reveled in the joy of discovery, and my gratitude was boundless (Klein, 1957, 251).

On the Power of Love

And so they talked on through the night, animated and happy. They faced what the morning would bring with the only weapon they had—their love for each other. Love is great, love is the foundation of nobility, it conquers obstacles and is a deep well of truth and strength. After hearing my parents talk that night I began to understand the greatness of their love. Their courage ignited within me a spark that continued to glow through the years of misery and defeat. The memory of their love—my only legacy—sustained me in happy and unhappy times in Poland, Germany, Czechoslovakia, France, Switzerland, Engand. It is still part of me, here in America (Klein, 1957, 86).

Important Dates

May 8, 1924	Gerda Weissmann Klein was born in Bielsko, Poland
September 3, 1939	The Germans occupied her town
October, 1939	Artur, Gerda's brother, ordered to a forced labor camp; Gerda never saw him again
Christmas, 1939	Gerda and her family ordered to live in the cold, damp basement of their home without water or electricity; remained there for two and a half years
June 28, 1942	"The worst day of my life," Gerda's father sent to a work camp
June 29, 1942	Gerda and her mother were seperated at the Bielsko train station and sent to different places; Gerda never

	saw her parents again. Gerda's mother went to Auschwitz. Gerda was sent to slave labor camps for the next three years.
January 29, 1945	Gerda and 2,000 other girls were subjected to a winter death march which lasted three months
May, 1945	The 120 surviviors and Gerda were placed in a vacant bicycle factory on the outskirts of Volary, Czechoslovakia where she was liberated by the American army; Gerda weighed 68 pounds, and her hair had turned gray
May 6, 1945	One of the first American soldiers Gerda met was Lieutenant Kurt Klien who would become her husband; Kurt, who was born in Germany, lost his parents in Auschwitz; Gerda later found out, where her parents also perished
June 18, 1946	Gerda and Kurt were married in Paris
September, 1946	Gerda and Kurt moved to Buffalo where Kurt was in the printing business
1957	First edition of *All But My Life* published by Hill and Wang; Gerda began her lifelong career of lecturing and writing about her experiences
1974	*The Blue Rose* was published
1981	Gerda's children's book on the Holocaust, *Promise of a New Spring*, published by Rossel Books
1984	*Passion for Sharing* was published and received a Valley Forge Award for Gerda
1996	*All But My Life* is in its 38th printing including a new, final chapter describing Gerda's life after liberation; the documentary story of her life, *One Survivor Remembers*, co-produced by HBO and the Holocaust Museum, wins an Oscar and an Emmy; Gerda gives an eloquent speech at the 1996 Academy Awards
January 2001	Gerda became a major healing voice in the Columbine High School tragedy through the charitable program she spawned; "The Heart of Columbine" is launched

2000   *The Hours After* is published by St. Martin's Press

Resources and References

Foster, H. M. 1997. "Embracing 'All But My Life' by Gerda Weissmann Klein." *English Journal*, 86: 56-59.

The Gerda and Kurt Klein Foundation www.kleinfoundation.org/main.html

Goodwin, D. K. 1994. *No Ordinary Time: Franklin and Eleanor Roosevelt the Home Front in World War II*. New York: Simon and Schuster.

Klein, G. W. 1957. *All But My Life*. New York: Hill and Wang.

Klein, G. W., & Klein, K. 2000. *The Hours After*. New York: St. Martin's Press.

Klein, G. W. 1981. *Promise of a New Spring*. Chappaqua, New York: Rossel Books.

Rubin, J. 2001. *Columbine: Two Years After*. Available from the Scholastic web site: (http://www.teacher.scholastic.com/newszone/specialreports/safety/columbine.htm)

A Survivor's Story: "Gerda Klein's life's work is to not let the world forget the horrors of the Holocaust," *Detroit News*, [cited September 9, 1996]. Available from World Wide Web: (www.detnews.com/1996/menu/stories/64217.html).

NOTES

Courtesy of The Albert Schweitzer Fellowship (www.schweitzerfellowship.org)

ALBERT SCHWEITZER
(1875-1965)

By Dan McBrayer

Albert Schweitzer was a young intellectual teaching at the University of Strassburg and pastoring a church when he read, by chance, an article that would change his life dramatically. The article addressed the need for medical missionaries in Africa. He previously had earned advanced degrees in philosophy, theology, and music but after reading this article he enrolled in medical school. Upon completion of his medical degree, at age thirty-eight, he embarked on a fifty-year career of service to the poor in Africa. The life and work of Schweitzer have become a universal symbol of altruism, self-sacrifice, and dedication. Dr. Schweitzer was one of the greatest humanitarians of the 20th century. He received the Nobel Prize for Peace in 1952.

> It is not out of goodness towards others that I am gentle, peace loving, long suffering and friendly, but because by being so I ultimately sustain my deepest self.

Key Themes in Schweitzer's Life

Albert Schweitzer was always a risk taker who possessed a big heart, an exceptional intellect, and very diverse interests. His life was spent in service to others, in pursuit of truth, and attempting to make the world a better place in every regard. He showed deep, intellectual concern for the problems of the human spirit. There are four themes that characterize Schweitzer's life: (a) he struggled with the idea of whether we had the *right* to good fortune; (b) he felt that moral and ethical leadership could best be provided by how we live our lives, not by what we profess about these issues; (c) his almost mystic Reverence for Life was a controlling feature of his philosophy, his work, and his legacy; and (d) he believed that we must remain loyal to our true selves and not give in to pressures to conform (and thus accept mediocrity). Each of these themes helps us understand how he would suggest that we "Get A Life."

Early Life Influences

Schweitzer was born in 1875 in Germany. His father was a pastor and a teacher, and his mother was the daughter of a pastor. Schweitzer did not have an atypical childhood, but there were several events he credited as "critical" in shaping who he would become. As a small boy, and the parson's son, he never felt totally accepted by the other village boys because they saw him as "better off." He struggled with this and even rejected nicer clothing so he would better fit in with the other school boys. He began to feel guilty because his family had more than others. These incidents may have left such an impression that Schweitzer would later forgo a comfortable life in Europe for his life of service to others in Africa.

When Schweitzer started school, he was awestruck by his first encounter with the school's administrator. This man had authored the two reading books that he and his classmates were using. He was so inspired by the encounter that he suspected the man must have had a halo! His suspicion was in reference to the fact that the only book Schweitzer respected more than these reading books was the *Bible*. The encounter with the school administrator may have impressed Schweitzer so much that he later became an author, in addition to his many other accomplishments.

While studying at the Gymnasium, (at about age 11) he became very passionate about reading. His passion was boundless, and it remained with him throughout his life. He would sometimes read all night—and then reread the book again. In addition to reading, he was "forced" to play the piano daily—another area of expertise he developed. He began playing the organ in church at age nine, and by age sixteen he was playing the organ for concert recitals.

Religion

His early life in the church was somewhat unique. His father was the pastor of a Protestant church that also served as the Catholic church. As a child he thought it was "beautiful" that in his village Protestants and Catholics shared the same building. He developed interest, understanding, and tolerance as a result of this experience. He was always hopeful for religious unity— which he felt we must strive for if we are truly Christians. He was so intrigued that he later focused his studies and became a pastor and a professor of religion. He became a prolific and somewhat controversial author on many issues within Christianity.

If Schweitzer were alive today, he would probably be quite concerned about the financial "waste" that exists in organized religion and also in how it seems to, at times, divide us, rather than unify us as God's creatures. He might want to have many different groups using the same facilities and use the "brick-and-mortar" money for true humanitarian work in the community. What a novel idea! What about his idea of religious unity? What's up with that? Again, maybe we have allowed our own unique, esoteric practices to divide, rather than unite, the Christian community.

The Good Life vs. Service

Schweitzer was always moved by the suffering in the world. As an adolescent he began to struggle with the notion of his "good life." More specifically, he questioned whether we have a right to good fortune. These nagging issues became interwoven and largely determined his view of life and his future. He became motivated by the word of Jesus that we should not live our lives for ourselves. He decided, at age twenty-one, that his life would become, by age thirty, "direct service to humankind." During this nine-year period of soul searching he read, worked, and reflected on his mission for life. While teaching at the University of Strassburg (1904) and pastoring a church, he came by chance upon an article in the Paris Missionary Society's publication indicating their urgent need for physicians in the French Colony of Gabon (west coast of central Africa). This event ended his search! His life, his future, his mission became abundantly clear—he would become a physician and go to Africa as a medical missionary.

How to Live As a Role Model

Now that it was clear to him what he must do with his life, it almost became his "Quest for the Holy Grail." He developed the point of view that atonement for the wrongs that white Christians had done to underdeveloped countries/people was enough reason to justify missions. He taught and preached this theme for a year or so and then began making preparations to leave his professional career and enroll in medical school. He believed that, as a medical doctor, he could better serve the underprivileged people of Africa by putting the "religion of love" in practice with his hands as opposed to giving himself out in words as he had done in teaching and preaching.

Early life experiences had enabled Schweitzer to find meaning in life, individuality, and confidence. He urged others to follow their impulses. He was driven to "understand" everything he encountered. His inquisitiveness led him to read the great philosophers. He was inspired by many of them, but particularly the German writer, Goethe. He lived by this message from Goethe, "Strive for true humanity! Become yourself a man who is true to his inner nature, a man whose deed is in tune with his character" (Schweitzer, 1965, 18). What a great lesson in integrity. He also was inspired by "the most Christian Hindu of the century" Mohandas Gandhi. I wonder who inspires the majority of the youth of America today? Is it Goethe? Madonna? Hootie and the Blowfish?

Moral Leadership

Schweitzer was/is revered for the moral leadership he expressed in his books and in his life. His positions on religious, political, and social issues were sometimes controversial, but he was always true to himself and what he considered a higher authority. His decision to become a medical missionary was based partly on his desire for moral leadership. His studies in religion had led him to believe that his talents were a gift to be paid for by serving others. He felt that too many of his privileged peers in Europe were enjoying a level of happiness that was somewhat sinful and at the expense of others in our world who were suffering. He believed that man must discover and apply a universal ethic, which he labeled "Reverence for Life."

One of Schweitzer's views was that we must take the ethical religion of Jesus from His world-view and put it in practice in our own lives (Schweitzer, 1965). He believed we should make the Kingdom of God a reality in this world by works of love. By "works of love" Schweitzer meant service to others and reverence for life. In fact, a definition of ethics that has been attributed to him reads, "It is good to maintain life and further life; it is bad to damage and destroy life" (Schweitzer, 1965, 34). By serving poor blacks in Africa for fifty years he lived this philosophy!

Albert Schweitzer is considered by many people, in many countries, to be one of the foremost spiritual and ethical figures of the twentieth century. As a boy he thought deeply about life and what one should do with his time on earth. As a student he always dealt with the tough questions regarding religion, philosophy, and the meaning of life. As a young scholar he moved about the cultured circles of Europe with ease. As a medical missionary for the last half of his life, he left an impression and a legacy that has impacted millions of lives. He became a glowing exemplar of what man can be and do. As stated by Norman Cousins (1985), "The greatness of Schweitzer—indeed, the essence of Schweitzer—was the man as symbol" (303). His work is carried on in several states in America through the Schweitzer Fellows Program. The program focuses on idealism, inclusiveness, and the personal rewards of service to others.

Reverence for Life

At a very young age, Albert became saddened by the misery he saw around him. He demonstrated concern for all living things and prayed daily that God would protect all creatures that breathe. He even refused to hunt and fish because of what he saw as cruelty to God's creatures. It was through experiences like these that Schweitzer believed he gained strength and confidence as a person, because his peers would make fun of his kindness. Consequently, he started to follow his conscience rather than worry so much about "fitting in." His reverence for life seems almost fanatical at times, but upon further reflection it is a logical extension of what he pursued as a mission in life. He saw Reverence for Life as a totally new approach to ethics.

Schweitzer saw this Reverence for Life as inseparable from his highly moral and spiritual self.

> The deeper we look into nature, the more we recognize that it is full of life, and the more profoundly we know that all life is a secret and that we are united with all life that is in nature. Man can no longer live for himself alone. We realize that all life is valuable, and that we are united to all this life. From this knowledge comes our spiritual relationship to the universe (Schweitzer, 1947, 248).

> Ethics is nothing else than Reverence for Life. Reverence for Life affords me my fundamental principle of morality, namely, that good consists in maintaining, assisting and enhancing life. Affirmation of the will-to-live which appears in phenomenal form all around me, is only possible for me in that I give myself out for other life (Schweitzer, 1947, 259).

Family and Community

Schweitzer dearly loved his life work—possibly why he was so successful and productive until he was 90-years-old. He found his niche at age 38—so it is never too late. He brought his family into his mission and they lived and served together. His wife was a nurse, and his daughter operated the hospital after his death. Their work created a great sense of community and hope for the region of Africa in which they lived and toiled. This sense of community seems to have vanished from the lives of most Americans. We seem to be too busy creating a sense of "self." What has happened to the notion of interdependence?

A sense of community, whether local or global, was an issue for Schweitzer throughout his life. He spoke fondly of childhood experiences that shaped this dimension of his personality. The community of scholars in Europe was especially instrumental in his early adult development. During the last twenty years of his life (1945-1965) he became very concerned about the world community. He was especially concerned about the apparent drift in the world toward massive nuclear destruction. He communicated regularly on radio, in print, and in person to appeal to the world leaders for reason and caution. In his very humble and modest style he was very effective in helping to bring about a nuclear test-ban treaty. A July, 1963, telegram to Schweitzer from Norman Cousins reads: "NUCLEAR TEST BAN NOW IMMINENT. YOUR ROLE IN HELPING TO AROUSE WORLD PUBLIC OPINION ON THIS ISSUE WAS A KEY ONE IN THE PRESENT RESULT. YOU ARE ENTITLED TO THE APPRECIATION OF ALL HUMANITY." Much of his correspondence with Cousins, Eisenhower, Kennedy, Khrushchev, Nehru, etc. is public record.

Parallels?

There are probably other parallels to the life of Albert Schweitzer, but three unlikely, and diverse, examples would be the diversity of Theodore Roosevelt, the passion of the early civil rights activist W.E.B. Du Bois, and Schweitzer's friend Albert Einstein. Like Schweitzer, Roosevelt was a voracious reader, concerned about the environment, possessed many talents, and worked extremely hard. DuBois and Schweitzer lived in the same nine decades and fought for the under-privileged. DuBois was an educated man as well (First African-American Harvard Ph.D.) and served humanity with the same passion as Schweitzer. Einstein was born four years after Schweitzer, left a mark equally as great, was also a fervent pacifist, won a Nobel Prize, and looked very much like Schweitzer! Einstein once said of Schweitzer "he did not preach and did not warn and did not dream that his example would be an ideal and comfort to innumerable people—he simply acted out of inner necessity" (Mallin, n.d). Each of these men could have chosen numerous less stressful and more comfortable careers/lives, but that is not how they believed we should "Get A Life."

Be Yourself

The life of Albert Schweitzer should teach us many things. He thought and cared deeply. He was a lifelong learner. He combined religion, family, and work in a meaningful way. He was a servant to his God and fellow man. He worked for world peace and understanding. He led a full and fulfilled life. He was his own person. He did not worry about being "politically correct!" He positively influenced millions of people throughout the world. He left a legacy with his life, his example, and his writings. Albert Schweitzer truly maximized his potential.

Schweitzer's advice on how to live life is captured in the following lengthy quote from Memoirs of Childhood and Youth. He laments about maintaining one's youthfulness and not becoming trapped in the handcuffs of culture when he writes:

> The conviction that we have to struggle to remain as alive in our thinking and feeling as we were in our youth has accompanied me through life as a faithful mentor. Instinctively I have fought against becoming what is called a "mature person."
>
> The word "mature" applied to human beings was, and still is, somewhat uncanny to me. I hear within it, like musical discords, the words impoverishment, stunted growth, and blunted feelings.
>
> What is usually considered maturity in a person is really resigned reasonableness. It is acquired by adopting others as models and by abandoning one after another the thoughts and convictions that were dear to us in our youth. We believed in the good; we no longer do so. We had faith in the power of kindness and peaceableness; we have it no longer. We could be filled with enthusiasm; we can no longer be. In order to navigate more safely through the dangers and storms of life, we lightened our boat. We threw overboard goods that we thought were dispensable; but it was our food and water that we got rid of. Now we travel more lightly, but we are starving.
>
> In my youth I listened to conversations of grownups which wafted to me a breath of melancholy, depressing my heart. My elders looked back at the idealism and enthusiasm of their youth as something precious that they should have held on to. At the same time, however, they considered it sort of a law of nature that one cannot do that. This talk aroused in me the fear that I, too, would look back upon myself with such nostalgia. I decided never to submit to this tragic reasonableness. What I promised myself in almost boyish defiance I have tried to carry out.
>
> The maturity to which we are called means becoming ever simpler, ever more truthful, ever purer, ever more peaceful, ever gentler, ever kinder, and ever more compassionate. We do not have to surrender to any other limitation of our idealism. Thus the soft iron of youthful idealism hardens into the steel of adult idealism which will never be lost (Schweitzer 1997, 89-90, 93).

By all accounts Schweitzer lived his life in accordance with the above words. Many of his European colleagues, from childhood through his medical missionary work, questioned his decisions to go against the grain. He saw what conformity and regimentation could do to diminish the human spirit, so he worked against it in his own life. His motto *Reverence for Life* is well documented and a manifestation of what he did for fifty years in Africa. His life of service to others speaks volumes for how we may choose to align our priorities.

When the Road is Smooth

Above all, we should not accept this smoothness as our *right*! We must work for what we have. One of Schweitzer's habits was intense thought—introspection. In good times he would invite us to be humble, plan ahead, be grateful for our blessings, and reach out to others. This is the time to reflect and regenerate. "The great secret of success is to go through life as a man who never gets used up" (Schweitzer 1947, 132).

When the Road Gets Rocky

Anyone who proposes to do good must not expect people to roll stones out of his way, but must accept his lot calmly if they even roll a few more upon it. A strength which becomes clearer and stronger through its experience of such obstacles is the only strength that can conquer them. Resistance is only a waste of strength (Schweitzer 1933, 112).

When You Encounter a Dragon in the Middle of the Road

Don't kill it! Schweitzer's Reverence for Life includes *all* life. Obviously, if his life or the life of others was seriously threatened he may become a "dragon slayer." However, if there was any way to co-exist he would give up a great deal so the dragon could live. As a Christian humanist he would profess that we must afford every creature's will-to-live the same Reverence for Life that we give our own. He believed that being good was preserving and promoting life; and that being evil was to destroy, injure or repress any life that may be capable of development. This belief is a part of his universal ethic which seeks to relieve all suffering.

The Crux: Schweitzer's Advice for Getting a Life

1. Be willing to ask the tough questions and work diligently to seek answers.
2. Read/study in a variety of areas and with depth.
3. Think for yourself and avoid the trap of conformity and regimentation.
4. Be a reasoned risk taker.
5. Love and respect the value and possibilities of all life.
6. We do not have the *right* to good fortune. We must work for it.
7. Moral and ethical leadership can best be provided by how we live our lives.
8. Share your gifts/talents with others and give back to the world some of what was given to you by God and man.
9. "Truth has no special time of its own. Its hour is now—always."
10. "The purpose of human life is to serve and to show compassion and the will to help others."

In a Nutshell

Here was a man who, in the 90 years of his productive life, had earned doctorates in the fields of philosophy, theology, music, and medicine, and was famous in each; who had almost single-handedly built and established a hospital for natives in the heart of equatorial Africa; who was awarded, in 1952, the Nobel Prize for Peace; who was recognized as an authority of the interpretations and playing of Johann Sebastian Bach's music; who wrote controversial books on the life of Jesus; and whose two volume study, *The Philosophy of Civilization*, was honored as a monument to penetrating thought and lofty ideals (Negri 1993, 26).

The Wisdom of Albert Schweitzer

On Attitudes
The greatest discovery of any generation is that human beings can alter their lives by altering their attitudes....

On Responsibility

Life outside a person is an extension of the life within. This compels us to be a part of it and to accept responsibility for all creatures great and small.

On Reverence for Life

The laying down of the commandment not to kill and not to damage is one of the greatest events in the spiritual history of mankind.

Just as white light consists of colored rays, so Reverence for Life contains all the components of ethics: love, kindliness, sympathy, empathy, peacefulness, power to forgive."

On Ethics

Only a humanity which is striving after ethical ends can in full measure share in the blessings brought by material progress and become master of the dangers which accompany it.

On Peace

The highest insight man can attain is the yearning for peace, for the union of his will with an infinite will, his human will with God's will.

On the Influence of One Life

Not one of us knows what effect his life produces, and what he gives to others; that is hidden from us and must remain so, though we are often allowed to see some little fraction of it, so that we may not lose courage. The way in which power works is a mystery.

On Doing the Right Thing

Humanitarian work should call on the people as such and not on their capacity as members of any particular church or nation.

Truth is always gain, however hard it is to accommodate ourselves to it.

Important Dates

1875	Born in Alsace (then part of Germany)
1884	Began playing organ for church services
1893-98	Studied theology, philosophy, and musical theory at University of Strassburg
1898-99	Studied at the Sorbonne in Paris
1899-1912	Earned three Doctorates, taught, preached.
1900-1965	Lectured all over the world and received numerous awards/metals/recognitions
1906-1913	Medical school at Strassburg
1912	Married Helene Bresslau (a nurse)
1913-1965	Established and operated hospital in Africa
1952	Received Nobel Peace Prize
1965	Died at his hospital in Lambarene, Africa
2001	88th anniversary of the hospital at Lambarene

References and Resources

Cousins, N. 1985. *Albert Schweitzer's Mission: Healing and Peace.* New York: W. W. Norton and Company.

Mallin, L. B. n.d. *Albert Schweitzer 1875-1965* [cited January, 22, 2001]. Available from the World Wide Web: (http://www.schweitzerfellowship.org/new-page4.html).

Negri, M. 1993. "The Humanism of Albert Schweitzer." *Humanist*, 53(2): 26.

Schweitzer, A. 1997. *Memoirs of Childhood and Youth.* Syracuse, NY: Syracuse University Press.

Schweitzer, A. 1933. *Out of My Life and Thought: An Autobiography.* New York: Henry Holt and Company.

Schweitzer, A. 1955. *The Philosophy of Civilization.* New York: The Macmillan Company.

Schweitzer, A. 1965. *Reverence for Life.* New York: Philosophical Library.

Schweitzer, A. 1947. *The Spiritual Life.* Boston: The Beacon Press.

NOTES

A/P World Wide Photos

OPRAH WINFREY

(1954-)

By Bob Frank

Oprah Winfrey's broadcasting career began when she was a teenager in Nashville, reading news for a local radio station. While attending Tennessee State University, she was news anchor for Nashville's WTVF television station. Only a few hours shy of graduation, she accepted a job in Baltimore as a news reporter for WJZ-TV. The station soon found her talents better suited to a morning talk show, which she co-hosted. In 1984, Oprah moved to Chicago to take over the flagging "A.M. Chicago" talk show. Within a year, Oprah was trouncing Phil Donahue's nationally syndicated talk show in the ratings, and the show was renamed "The Oprah Winfrey Show." Shortly thereafter, the show was nationally syndicated and Oprah became a household name. During the same year, 1985, Oprah was nominated for an academy award for her role as Sophia in The Color Purple. *Today, Oprah reigns as a media titan. She owns her talk show, the studio in which it is taped, her production company, and a substantial share of the company that syndicates her show, King World Productions. She also produces and acts in movies, started her own magazine,* O, *and an interactive cable channel,* Oxygen Media, Inc. *With a net worth above $1 billion, she is the first black billionaire. Throughout all her media enterprises Oprah has maintained a consistent message: people have to take personal responsibility for their lives in order to be fulfilled.*

Most of the world is operating on somebody else's definition of what they should be and all I'm here to do is help people remember: Define yourself (Lynch, 1998, 4).

Take Charge of Your Life

Oprah Winfrey has always been clear about her message. It is a message that permeates her talk show, book club, film productions, cable channel, magazine—every outlet at her disposal. The message is quite simple: you are responsible for your life. The greatest lesson of her own life, she says, is "to recognize that I am solely responsible for it, and not trying to please other people, and not living my life to please other people, but doing what my heart says all the time" (American Academy of Achievement [AAA], 1997). Individuals need to learn to take charge of their lives; they have "to realize that things are not just happening to them willy-nilly" (AAA, 1997). Once you figure out your vision for life, once you define yourself, you will find that doors miraculously begin to open, and "the universe will respond" (Zents, 1995).

Listen to Your Own Voice

Crucial to defining yourself is the ability to filter through the competing voices of others telling you what to do and how to live your life. "The voices of the world will drown out the voice of God and your intuition if you let it. And most people are directed by voices outside themselves" (AAA, 1997).

One of the greatest barriers to hearing your own voice is the ingrained attitude most of us have that we must instantly please everyone else that we can never let others, especially our friends, down. Oprah counsels that an obsession with pleasing others is a sure path to an unhappy, unfulfilled life. One way to avoid this trap is to learn to say no to others, even your friends, and not feel guilty about it. Another is to never forget that you have the right to change your mind. You alone are the master of your own destiny. You—no one else—will be held accountable on Judgment Day.

Importance of Gratitude

Among the jangle of interfering voices in our lives are those telling us we haven't gotten all we want yet. We have too little, too little time, too little money, too little success. What we tend to focus on is what we don't have. So long as that is our focus, we can never live in the moment. Our superficial desires obscure the inner voice of our dreams and intuitions. That is why Oprah urges us to focus instead on what we have rather than on what we lack.

One way to live in the moment is to keep a "grateful journal." Every night before going to bed, write down five things that happened that you are grateful for—good, fulfilling, happy events, no matter how small. Focus upon these positives, rather than fears, failures, or longings. As a result, positive thoughts will surge to the fore of our consciousness without any effort. We have the power to direct our thoughts toward constructive ends.

Give Back What You Can

One of the greatest influences on Oprah's life was her grandmother, Hattie Mae Bullock. In ways too numerous to count, Hattie Mae impressed upon her granddaughter the importance of one of her favorite Bible verses, Romans 15:1: "We then that are strong ought to bear the infirmities of the weak." Not only has Oprah dedicated her powerful voice to a mission to help others liberate themselves, a spirit of philanthropy and service permeates her efforts in and out of the studio.

Neither her fame nor her fortune determines Oprah's sense of success. As she once told the graduates of Wesleyan (paraphrasing Dr. King), "Greatness is determined by service" (Lowe, 1998, 76). Oprah serves the African-American community through powerful films that give voice to their silent past and through millions of dollars of donations to black colleges. She is an ardent supporter of Habitat for Humanity, Boys and Girls Clubs, and countless other charitable organizations.

Get Over It

Telling her tens of millions of listeners to take responsibility for their lives is a hard sell in an era when we look for victims behind every neurosis.

Hardened criminals are victims of childhood abuse; the rising number of unwed mothers is due to neglect and poverty; accidents simply don't happen anymore—your injury is always someone else's fault.

But don't tell any of this to Oprah. As the controversial but popular Dr. Laura said of her peer: "She's determined to be the architect of her own life. And she doesn't use the past as the basis for her identity" ("No Guts," 1991, 76). If anyone had a past that could be mined for rich veins of victimology, it is Oprah. Born out of wedlock into poverty, shuffled cross-country from the care of her grandmother to her mother then to her father, molested and raped by relatives in her teens, Oprah even gave birth to a premature baby who died soon after. Yet Oprah never used her past as an excuse.

Oprah believes that if you define yourself according to your past, you confine yourself. As she puts it: "I don't think of myself as a poor ghetto girl who made good. I think of myself as somebody who from an early age knew I was responsible for myself, and I had to make good" (Saidman, 1990, 42). As she would tell anyone, much of her success in triumphing over a difficult past is due to the steady and stern discipline provided first by her grandparents, until age six, and then by her father Vernon after she turned fourteen.

Oprah perhaps put it best when she said, "Turn your wounds into wisdom. You will be wounded many times in your life. You'll make mistakes. Some people will call them failures, but I have learned that failure is really God's way of saying, 'Excuse me, you're moving in the wrong direction'" (Winfrey, 1997).

The Power of Reading

From an early age Oprah Winfrey recognized the power of the spoken word. As a child she performed recitations at churches in rural Mississippi. In high school she excelled in public speaking competitions. She even received a public speaking scholarship to attend college. And her phenomenal success as the premier talk show host offers abundant testimony to the power of the spoken word in her own life.

But Oprah would be the first to acknowledge the primary importance of the written word. The initiation of her now-famous Book Club in 1996, although a risky programming idea for television, was a natural outgrowth of her love of reading. She has always been keenly aware of the impact of reading on her own life. Her first recollection of being validated came as a teenager, upon reading *I Know Why the Caged Bird Sings*, by Maya Angelou. "The fact that someone as poor as I, as black as I, from the South, from rape, from confusion could move to hope, to possibility, to victory—could be written about in a real book, that I had chosen in a library—was amazing to me. Authors could do that, with the word" ("Oprah Winfrey," July 16, 2000).

Reading gave Oprah hope, opened her eyes to the possibilities life had to offer. Reading is the bedrock of education, and an education through reading is one of the surest ways to defining yourself and attaining your dreams.

Oprahfication as Communication

The Oprah Winfrey Show reaches nearly fifteen million viewers daily in the United States, and is shown in over 130 countries. The winner of more than two dozen Emmys, it remains the most-watched talk show in America. So, what does the unparalleled success of a show have to do with the philosophy of its host?

In writing about Oprah's appeal, Deborah Tannen has noted that Oprah's early competitor, Phil Donahue, engaged in "report talk," which typifies men's conversation. Tannen writes, "The overt focus is on information. Winfrey transformed the format into what I call 'rapport talk,' the back-and-forth conversation that is the basis of female friendship, with its emphasis on self-revealing intimacies." The broader cultural effect of this unique format has culminated in a new word in the American lexicon: "Oprahfication." Oprahfication refers to the result of that give-and-take, self-revealing, highly confessional dialogue that characterizes an Oprah interview.

Oprah doesn't detail the earth-shaking events in the lives of people she interviews, not even the celebrities. Instead she relates to them as everyday folks, with everyday concerns that they both share aloud in front of the camera. Much of Oprah's mass appeal derives from this confessional style. Oprah is more like your sister than a media mogul. We can identify.

The power to connect gives wings to Oprah's central message—you really can define yourself, liberate yourself, by taking charge and becoming responsible for your own life. A message without wings is a message that falls flat to the earth. Oprah's unique communicative style has given wings to her message.

Biographical Sketch

Born in 1954 in rural Mississippi to unwed parents, Oprah Winfrey spent her first six years with her grandmother. She then went to live with her mother in Milwaukee until she was fourteen. By this time she had been raped by a cousin, had given birth to a baby who died within a week, and was heading for a career as a juvenile delinquent. Her father sent for her to come live with him in Nashville. Under the strict discipline of her father, Vernon, Oprah's entire life changed directions.

While still in high school, Oprah worked part-time at a local radio station. An accomplished public speaker, she won a partial scholarship for her speaking to Tennessee State University in 1971. Two years later, while still in school, she became the first black female anchor for a television news show in Nashville. Her success there at WTVF-TV led to an offer to anchor the 6 o'clock news at WJZ-TV in Baltimore in 1976. She left Tennessee State just a few hours shy of a degree in speech and performing arts. (She was awarded a diploma in 1987—after she completed the work for her senior project. Then she gave the commencement address.) It was not long before WJZ-TV "demoted" Oprah to co-host for a morning talk show, where her talent thrived. In 1984, she accepted the job as host of "A.M. Chicago." Her brilliant success in turning that show's ratings around led to a name change for the show within the year—"The Oprah Winfrey Show."

Over the years Oprah and her show soon won more than a dozen Emmys. She has won nearly every broadcasting award the industry offers, including, The George Foster Peabody Individual Achievement Award in 1996.

The success of the Oprah Winfrey show paved the way for her current multimedia empire. After Capitol Cities decided to buy her show from ABC, she went on to buy a production studio, create a production company (Harpo Productions, Inc.), and even became a major shareholder in the distributor of her show, King World Productions. Her parent company, Harpo Entertainment Group, also owns Oprah's new magazine, "*O*," and part of a women's cable channel, Oxygen Media.

Already a one-woman media conglomerate, Oprah shows no signs of slowing down. Her voice will be heard, loud and clear, for years to come.

When the Road is Smooth

So now my goal in life is not to have to hit the eye of the storm, but to catch it in the whisper. To get it the first time. I think the thing, the one thing that has allowed me to certainly achieve both material success and spiritual success, is the ability to listen to my instinct. I call it my inner voice (AAA, 1997).

When the Road Gets Rocky

Turn your wounds into wisdom. You will be wounded many times in your life. You'll make mistakes. Some people will call them failures but I have learned that failure is really God's way of saying, 'Excuse me, you're moving in the wrong direction.' It's just an experience, just an experience (Winfrey, 1997).

When You Encounter a Dragon in the Middle of the Road

Not all dragons are evil. Wait and see.
One of the biggest lessons I've learned recently is that when you don't know what to do, you should do nothing until you figure out what to do because a lot of times you feel like you are pressed against the wall, and you've got to make a decision. You don't have to do anything. Don't know what to do? Do nothing. I won't (AAA, 1997).

The Crux: Oprah's Ten Commandments for Success

1. Don't live your life to please others.
2. Don't depend on forces outside of yourself to get ahead.
3. Seek harmony and compassion in your business and personal life.
4. Get rid of the back-stabbers—surround yourself only with people who will lift you higher.
5. Be nice.
6. Rid yourself of your addictions—whether they are food, alcohol, drugs, or behavior habits.

7. Surround yourself with people who are as smart as or smarter than you.
8. If money is your motivation, forget it.
9. Never hand over your power to someone else.
10. Be persistent in pursuing your dreams (Lowe, 1998, 168-169).

In a Nutshell

I think that one of the most important lessons to learn is that we are all responsible for our own lives. But nobody gets through this alone. Everybody needs somebody to show them a way out, or a way up (AAA, 1997).

The Wisdom of Oprah Winfrey

On Being Grateful

I believe that if you can learn to focus on what you have, you will always see that the universe is abundant and you will have more. If you concentrate and focus in your life on what you don't have, you will never have enough. Be grateful. Keep a journal (Oprah Winfrey, July 16, 2000).

On Happiness

I've realized it's very simple things that make me happy, but that I have to be open to happiness. I have to want to be happy rather than just busy. And once I am more willing to be happy, it becomes easier for one to feel the happiness (Cleage, 1991, 48).

On Saying "No"

I think the lesson that you learn from allowing yourself to be abused as a child is an ongoing lesson. What I recognize is that the same thing, in some cases, that causes a child to be abused, is the same thing that causes you to be abused as an adult. It is the same thing in your adulthood that allows you to never be able to say 'No' to people (AAA, 1997).

On Pleasing Others

Most all the mistakes I've made in my life, I've made because I was trying to please other people. Every one of them...every mistake

I've ever made was because I went outside myself to do something for somebody else that I should not have (AAA, 1997).

On Work

The process of the work is far more important to me, in many cases, than the end result. Once the picture is finished, that's fine. The process of working on a show and being in the midst of a show—being right in the heart of it—is far more stimulating, fulfilling, and exciting to me than finishing the show (AAA, 1997).

On Education

For me, education is about the most important thing because that is what liberated me. Education is what liberated me. The ability to read saved my life (AAA, 1997).

On Good Management

To me, one of the most important things about being a good manager is to rule with a heart. You have to know the business, but you also have to know what's at the heart of the business, and that's the people. People matter (Reynolds, 1995, 15).

Important Dates

1954	Born on January 29 in Kosciusko, Mississippi.
1971	Enrolled in Tennessee State University to study speech and performing arts.
1972	Named Miss Black Tennessee.
1976	Joined Baltimore's WJZ-TV News.
1977	Became co-host of WJZ-TV's *People Are Talking*.
1984	Became host of WLS-TV's *A.M. Chicago*.
1985	*A.M. Chicago* is renamed *The Oprah Winfrey Show*.
1985	Nominated for Academy Award for Best Supporting Actress for role as Sophia in *The Color Purple*.
1986	*The Oprah Winfrey Show* became nationally syndicated.
1986	Formed HARPO Productions, Inc.
1988	Received International Radio and Television Society's "Broadcaster of the Year" award.
1988	HARPO Productions, Inc. buys *The Oprah Winfrey Show* from Capitol Cities/ABC.

1996	Received George Foster Peabody Individual Achievement Award.
1996	Began Oprah's Book Club.
1996	Named by *Time Magazine* one of 25 most influential people in the world.
1997	Launched Oprah's Angel Network.
1998	Named one of the 100 Most Influential People of the 20th Century by *Time*.
1998	Received National Academy of Television Arts and Science Lifetime Achievement Award.
1998	Launched Oxygen Media, Inc., a cable channel for women.
1998	Premier of film *Beloved*.
1999	Began teaching as adjunct professor at Northwestern University's Kellogg Graduate School of Management.
2000	Introduced *O*, the Oprah Magazine.

References and Resources

About Oprah. 2000. Available from the World Wide Web: (http://oprah.com/about/aboutharpo/about_harpo_main.html)

Adler, B. ed. 1997. *The Uncommon Wisdom of Oprah Winfrey: A Portrait in Her Own Words.* Seacaucus, N.J.: Citadel Press.

American Academy of Achievement. 1997. Oprah Winfrey: Biography; interview. Available from the World Wide Web: (http://www.achievement.org/autodoc/page/winObio)

Cleage, P. 1991. "Walking in the Light." *Essence* [Quoted in Lowe, 71].

Clemetson, L. 2001. "Oprah on Oprah." *Newsweek* (January 8):38-43.

Lowe, J. 1998. *Oprah Winfrey Speaks: Insight From the World's Most Influential Voice.* New York: John Wiley and Sons, Inc.

Lynch, L. 1998. Oprah's new mission. Available from the World Wide Web: (http://www.usaweekend.com/98_issues/981011/981011oprah.html)

Mair, G. 1994. *Oprah Winfrey: The Real Story.* Secaucus, N.J.: Birch Lane Press.

"No Guts, No Glory: Oprah as Survivor." *McCalls.* (August 1995).

2000. "Oprah Winfrey: A Thriving Survivor," (July 16). Available from the World Wide Web: (http://incestabuse.about.com/library/weekly/aa071600.htm?terms=Oprah)

Reynolds, G. 1995. "A Year to Remember: Oprah Grows Up," *TV Guide* (January 7): quoted in Lowe, p. 65.

Saidman, A. 1990. *Oprah Winfrey: Media Success Story.* Minneapolis: Lerner Publication.

Tannen, D. 1998. "The TV Host Oprah Winfrey." *Time*. Available from World Wide
    Web: (http://www.time.com/time100/artists/profile/winfrey.html)
Winfrey, O. 1997. Oprah Winfrey's commencement address, Wellesley College.
    Available from the World Wide Web:
    (http://www.Wellesley.edu/PublicAffairs/PAhomepage/winfrey.html)
Zents, B. 1995. "Light in People's Lives: Talk Show Host Emphasizes Vision,
    Helping Others," *Daily Illini*, April 4. Available from the World Wide Web:
    (http://www.dailyillini.com/archives/1995/April/4/oprah-p1/html)

NOTES

Courtesy of http://www.flyvision.org/sbm/bia.html

SIDDHARTHA GAUTAMA THE BUDDHA (566 BCE-486 BCE)

By George Boeree

The Buddha was born Siddhartha Gautama, a prince of the Sakya tribe of Nepal, in approximately 566 BCE. When he was twenty-nine years old, he left the comforts of his home to seek the meaning of the suffering he saw around him. After six years of arduous yogic training, he abandoned the way of self-mortification and instead sat in mindful meditation beneath a bodhi tree.

On the full moon of May, with the rising of the morning star, Siddhartha Gautama became the Buddha, which means "one who has awakened." The Buddha wandered the plains of northeastern India for 45 years more, teaching the path, or Dharma, he had realized in that moment. Around him developed a community, or Sangha, of monks and, later, nuns, drawn from every tribe and caste, devoted to practicing this path. In approximately 486 BCE, at the age of 80, the Buddha died. His last words are said to be, "Impermanent are all created things; Strive on with awareness!"

The path that Buddha founded has influenced innumerable lives in countless ways. Buddhism is a religion, a rich philosophy, and a way of life.

Buddhism has been adopted by and adapted to many different cultures, including (in the last century) the cultures of the west.

I teach suffering and the end of suffering.

When he left his family and home, Siddhartha's (the Buddha's) goal was to discover the causes of suffering and the means to eliminate them. In his very first sermon, he outlined the Four Noble Truths. Together, they form the framework for Buddhism, in all its forms.
1. Life is full of suffering.
2. Suffering is due to attachment.
3. Attachment can be overcome.
4. There is a path of transcendence that leads to the cessation of suffering called the Dharma. Buddha also called it the Middle Way, meaning the middle way between living a life of hedonistic abandon and living one of extreme asceticism and self-mortification.

The Middle Path

A description of how to live "the middle way" may be found in the thousands of sutras, Buddha's sermons. Many sutras are directed at monks and nuns, and can be quite demanding, from a modern perspective. But many are also directed at the general populace, referred to as "householders" in the sutras. Because the householder's mind may be cluttered with thoughts of family obligations, a job, and other worldly responsibilities, Buddha said it was more difficult for a householder to gain enlightenment. To gain enlightenment, one must pursue a life of morality, meditation, and wisdom.

Morality

Buddhists must follow five moral precepts:
1. Avoid killing or harming any person and, if possible, any living thing.
2. Avoid stealing—taking what is not yours to take.
3. Avoid sexual irresponsibility, which means celibacy for monks and nuns, and fidelity for the rest of us.

4. Avoid lying, or any hurtful speech such as gossip or ridicule.
5. Avoid alcohol and drugs, which diminish clarity of consciousness.

The law of nature regarding morality is called karma. Karma means that the evil you do will have repercussions that will, in the end, hurt you. Likewise, the good you do will somehow find its way back to you. Since most Buddhists also believe in some kind of reincarnation or rebirth, your karma follows you into future lives, hindering you or helping you on the path to enlightenment. As human beings, we should all make a daily effort to attain an optimal state of being.

Meditation

Meditation is often associated with Buddhism, especially among monks and nuns. However, householders may meditate as well, if not quite so often or as proficiently as those who have forsaken worldly goods for a life of contemplation. Meditation has two functions: on the one hand, meditation helps calm the overly active mind. We do this by sitting quietly and allowing our perceptions, thoughts, images, and feelings to come as they will—and drift back out. The idea is to not attach oneself to the things that come into mind, but to barely notice them. For example, if the thought "I really can't be late for the meeting" comes into your awareness, notice it ("ah, there's a thought!") but don't get involved in it. Let it go!

A second function of meditation is mindfulness. The "goal" of meditation is not to be aware of nothing, but to be aware of everything in a non-attached sort of way. So, as you acquire the ability to still your mind through meditation, you also allow it to open up. You need no longer fear that the barking dog or concerns about the neighbors will disturb your peace of mind. You hear the dog, you notice the thought. They are okay just as they are. They are life.

Buddha taught his son (Rahula) a simple form of meditation called "following your breath." Allow your breathing to fill your awareness, not in the sense of making comments about it in your head, but as something you are enjoying, as you might gaze at a sunset. When distractions come to mind, tip your hat to them and go back to "gazing" at your breathing.

Wisdom

Wisdom takes time. When we are young, we learn to repeat certain sayings to ourselves and others, understanding in a cognitive sense what they mean. Only over time do meanings sink in, do we feel the meanings in our hearts or our guts and not just in our brains. Only with age does knowledge become wisdom. Wisdom begins with the understanding that life is filled with suffering and that suffering comes from clinging, hatred, and ignorance. Morality and meditation are two of the forces that help us to "blow out" clinging, hatred, and ignorance. Wisdom is the third force.

We especially need to understand that as life is imperfect, so are individual human beings. So, a man and woman who get married should not expect perfection from their partner because perfection is not attainable in this world. When one mate discovers that the other snores, spends all day watching sports, wastes too much money on clothes, or burps at the dinner table, he or she may feel resentful or disappointed. They will say to themselves, "What did I ever see in him?" or "I could have done better than her!" Decency, rather than perfection, would seem a more attainable and practical attribute for a mate.

Wisdom also means coming to terms with impermanence. The minutes it takes to read this chapter have already disappeared into the past. As a parent, a baby may bring joy, but infancy, like all stages in life, is impermanent. A baby transforms into a toddler, a teenager, an adult. Nothing lasts forever.

Last, there is the idea that all things are interconnected and interdependent, that nothing is independent of anything else. From this perspective, everything that has happened in our lives, including mistakes and moments of sheer misery, has made us who we are. Similarly, everything we do and say today will have an impact on us and on others. Buddha uses the idea of reincarnation to elaborate on the interconnectedness of life:

> Rebirth began an inconceivably long time ago. No beginning is apparent. Beings suffering from ignorance and clinging continue to be born, and die, and be born again. A being who was not your mother once upon a time is not easy to find. A being who was not your father, your brother, your sister, your son, or your daughter once upon a time is not easy to find (The Mother Sutra, SN XV 14-19, interpreted).

Biographical Sketch of Siddhartha Gautama

There was a small country in what is now southern Nepal that was ruled by a clan called the Shakyas. The head of this clan, and the king of this country, was named Shuddodana Gautama, and his wife was the beautiful Mahamaya. Mahamaya was expecting her first born. She had had a strange dream in which a baby elephant had blessed her with his trunk, an auspicious sign.

As was the custom of the day, when the time came near for Queen Mahamaya to have her child, she traveled to her father's kingdom for the birth. But during the long journey, her birth pains began. In the small town of Lumbini, she asked her handmaidens to assist her to a nearby grove of trees for privacy. One large tree lowered a branch to her to serve as a support for her delivery. The birth was almost painless, even though the child had to be delivered from her side. After the birth, a gentle rain fell on the mother and the child to cleanse them.

It is said that the child was born fully awake and could speak right away. He told his mother he had come to free all mankind from suffering. He could stand, and he walked a short distance in each of the four directions. Lotus blossoms rose in his footsteps. They named him Siddhartha, which means "he who has attained his goals." Sadly, his mother (Mahamaya) died only seven days after the birth. Subsequently, Siddhartha was raised by his mother's kind sister, Mahaprajapati Gotami.

King Shuddodana consulted Asita, a well-known soothsayer, concerning the future of his son. Asita proclaimed that he would be one of two things: he could become a great king, even an emperor, or he could become a great sage and savior of humanity. The king, eager that his son should become a king like himself, was determined to shield the child from anything that might result in him taking up the religious life. And so Siddhartha was kept in the palaces, and was prevented from experiencing the commonplace. He was not permitted to see the elderly, the sickly, the dead, or anyone who had dedicated themselves to spiritual practices. Only beauty and health surrounded Siddhartha.

Siddhartha grew up to be a strong and handsome young man. As a prince of the warrior caste, he trained in the arts of war. When it came time for him to marry, he won the hand of a beautiful princess of a neighboring kingdom by besting all competitors at a variety of sports. Yashodhara was her name, and they married when both were 16 years old.

As Siddhartha continued living in the luxury of his palaces, he grew increasing restless and curious about the world beyond the palace walls. He finally demanded that he be permitted to see his people and his lands. The king carefully arranged that Siddhartha should still not see the kind of suffering that he feared would lead him to a religious life, and decreed that only young and healthy people should greet the prince.

As he was led through Kapilavatthu, the capital, he chanced to see a couple of old men who had accidentally wandered near the parade route. Amazed and confused, he chased after them to find out what they were. Then he came across some people who were severely ill. And finally, he came across a funeral ceremony by the side of a river, and for the first time in his life, he saw death. He asked his friend and squire Channa the meaning of all these things, and Channa informed him of the simple truths that Siddhartha should have known all along—that we all get old, sick, and eventually die.

Siddhartha also saw an ascetic, a monk who had renounced all the pleasures of the flesh. The peaceful look on the monk's face would stay with Siddhartha for a long time to come.

At the age of 29, Siddhartha came to realize that he could no longer be content to live the life he had known. He had discovered suffering, and wanted more than anything to discover how one might overcome suffering. After kissing his sleeping wife and newborn son Rahula goodbye, he sneaked out of the palace with his squire Channa and his favorite horse Kanthaka. He gave away his rich clothing, cut his long hair, and gave the horse to Channa and told him to return to the palace. He studied for a while with two famous gurus of the day, but found their practices lacking.

He began to practice the austerities and self-mortifications of a group of five ascetics. For six years, he practiced, and the sincerity and intensity of his desire were so astounding that, before long, the five ascetics became his followers. Despite his efforts, the answers to his questions did not materialize. So, he redoubled his efforts, refusing food and water until he was in a state of near death.

One day, a peasant girl named Sujata saw him, a starving monk, and took pity on him. She begged him to eat some of her milk-rice. Siddhartha realized that his extreme practices were leading him nowhere, that in fact it might be better to find some middle way between the extremes of the life of luxury and the life of self-mortification. So, he ate, and drank, and bathed in the river. The five ascetics saw him and concluded that Siddhartha had given up the ascetic life and taken to the ways of the flesh.

In the town of Bodh Gaya, Siddhartha decided that he would sit under a certain fig tree as long as it would take for the answers to the problem of suffering to come. He sat there for many days, first in deep concentration to clear his mind of all distractions, then in mindfulness meditation, opening himself up to the truth. He began to recall all his previous lives and to see everything that was going on in the entire universe. On the full moon of May, with the rising of the morning star, Siddhartha finally understood the answer to the question of suffering and became the Buddha, which means "he who is awake."

It is said that Mara, the evil one, tried to prevent the great awakening. First, he tried to frighten Siddhartha with storms and armies of demons, but Siddhartha remained completely calm. Then, he sent his three beautiful daughters to tempt him, again to no avail. Finally, he tried to ensnare Siddhartha in his own ego by appealing to his pride. That, too, failed. Siddhartha, having conquered all temptations, touched the ground with one hand and asked the earth to be his witness. Siddhartha, now the Buddha, remained seated under the tree—which we call the bodhi tree—for many days longer. It seemed to him that this knowledge he had gained was far too difficult to communicate to others. Legend has it that Brahma, king of the gods, convinced Buddha to teach, saying that some of us perhaps have only a little dirt in our eyes and could awaken if we only heard his story. Buddha agreed to teach.

At Sarnath near Benares, about one hundred miles from Bodh Gaya, he came across the five ascetics he had practiced with for so long. There, in a deer park, he preached his first sermon, which is called "setting the wheel of the teaching in motion." He explained to them the Four Noble Truths and the Eight Fold Path. They became his very first disciples and the beginnings of the Sangha or community of monks. His aunt and wife asked to be permitted into the Sangha, which was originally composed only of men. The culture of the time ranked women far below men in importance, and at first it seemed that permitting women to enter the community would weaken it. But the Buddha relented, and his aunt and wife became the first Buddhist nuns.

The Buddha said that it didn't matter what a person's status in the world was, or what their background or wealth or nationality might be. All were capable of enlightenment, and all were welcome into the Sangha. The first ordained Buddhist monk, Upali, had been a barber, yet he was ranked higher than monks who had been kings because he had taken his vows earlier than they.

Buddha achieved his enlightenment at the age of 35. He would teach throughout northeast India for another 45 years. When the Buddha was 80 years old, he told his friend and cousin Ananda that he would be leaving them soon. And so it came to be that in Kushinagara, not a hundred miles from his homeland, he ate some spoiled food and became very ill. He went into a deep meditation under a grove of sala trees and died.

When the Road is Smooth

Thousands of candles can be lighted from a single candle, and the life of the candle will not be shortened. Happiness never decreases by being shared.

When the Road Gets Rocky

Upon a heap of rubbish in the roadside ditch, blooms a lotus, fragrant and pleasing (From the Dhammapada, 4-58).

When You Encounter a Dragon in the Middle of the Road

Like a falling star, like a bubble in a stream,
Like a flame in the wind, like frost in the sun,
Like a flash of lightning or a passing dream—
So should you understand the world of the ego
(From the Diamond Sutra).

The Crux

To do no evil.
To cultivate good.
To purify one's mind.
These are the teachings of the Buddha
(from The Dhammapada, 14.183).

In a Nutshell

The Buddha taught that by making a serious effort at a moral life, by cultivating our minds with meditation, and by gaining the wisdom contained in Buddha's teaching, we can become better, happier, and more compassionate people.

> By oneself is evil done; by oneself is one defiled. By oneself is evil left undone; by oneself is one made pure. Purity and impurity depend on oneself; no one can purify another (The Dhammapada, 12.165).

The Wisdom of the Buddha

On Hatred

Hatred is never appeased by hatred in this world. By non-hatred alone is hatred appeased. This is a law eternal (From The Dhammapada 1.5).

On Criticizing Others

Let none find fault with others; let none see the omissions and commissions of others. But let one see one's own acts, done and undone (4.50).

Easily seen is the fault of others, but one's own fault is difficult to see. Like chaff, one winnows another's faults, but hides one's own, even as a crafty fowler hides behind sham branched (18.252).

On Self Delusion

A fool who knows his foolishness is wise at least to that extent, but a fool who thinks himself wise is a fool indeed (5.63).

On Overcoming Obstacles

Overcome the angry by non-anger; overcome the wicked by goodness; overcome the miser by generosity; overcome the liar by truth (17.223).

On Self-Pity

The Buddha said, "When touched with a feeling of pain, the unenlightened person sorrows, grieves, laments, beats his chest, and becomes distraught. So now he feels two pains, physical and mental. It is just as if someone were to shoot a man with an arrow and, right afterward, shoot him with another one, so he would feel the pains of two arrows!" (from the Sutra of the Arrow SN XXXVI.6, interpreted).

On Anger

An angry person is ugly and sleeps poorly. Gaining a profit, he turns it into a loss, having done damage with word and deed. A person overwhelmed with anger destroys his wealth. Maddened with anger, he destroys his status. Relatives, friends, and colleagues avoid him. Anger brings loss. Anger inflames the mind. He doesn't realize that his danger is born from within. An angry person doesn't know his own benefit. An angry person doesn't see the Dharma. A man conquered by anger is in a mass of darkness. He takes pleasure in bad deeds as if they were good, but later, when his anger is gone, he suffers as if burned with fire. He is spoiled, blotted out, like fire enveloped in smoke.

When anger spreads, when a man becomes angry, he has no shame, no fear of evil, is not respectful in speech. For a person overcome with anger, nothing gives light (From the Sutra of the Angry Person, AN VII.60).

On the Good Life

(Buddha's aunt, wishing to retreat into the forest to live alone, asked the Buddha what she should keep in mind.)

Gotami, qualities that you know lead to disturbance rather than calm, to being fettered rather than being unfettered, to accumulating things rather than shedding them, to self-important rather than to modesty, to discontent rather than contentment, to entanglement in the world rather than seclusion, to laziness rather than to persistence, to being burdensome rather than being unburdensome, those qualities are not the way. Those qualities you know to lead to calm rather than disturbance, to being unfettered rather than being fettered, to shedding things rather than accumulating them, to modesty rather than self-importance, to contentment rather than discontent, to seclusion rather than entanglement, to persistence rather than laziness, to being unburdensome rather than burdensome, those qualities are indeed the way (from Gotami's Sutra, AN VIII.53, interpreted).

On Trusting your Instincts

Come, people, do not base your life on what others tell you, nor
upon tradition, nor upon rumor, nor upon scripture, nor upon sur-
mise, nor upon axioms, nor upon specious reasoning, nor upon
some bias, nor upon someone's apparent talents, nor upon the
authority of a teacher. Instead, when you yourselves know 'These
things are good, these things are worthy, these things are wise,
these things lead to happiness and well-being,' then you should go
ahead and live life accordingly (from the Sutra of the Kalamas, AN
III.65, interpreted).

On Kindness

This is what should be done
By one who is skilled in goodness,
And who knows the path of peace:
Let them be able and upright,
Straightforward and gentle in speech.
Humble and not conceited,
Contented and easily satisfied.
Unburdened with duties and frugal in their ways.
Peaceful and calm, and wise and skillful,
Not proud and demanding in nature.
Let them not do the slightest thing
That the wise would later reprove.
Wishing: In gladness and in safety,
May all beings be at ease.
Whatever living beings there may be;
Whether they are weak or strong, omitting none,
The great or the mighty, medium, short or small,
The seen and the unseen,
Those living near and far away,
Those born and to-be-born,
May all beings be at ease!
Let none deceive another,
Or despise any being in any state.
Let none through anger or ill-will
Wish harm upon another.
Even as a mother protects with her life
Her child, her only child,
So with a boundless heart
Should one cherish all living beings:
Radiating kindness over the entire world
Spreading upwards to the skies,

And downwards to the depths;
Outwards and unbounded,
Freed from hatred and ill-will.
Whether standing or walking, seated or lying down
Free from drowsiness,
One should sustain this recollection.
This is said to be the sublime abiding.
By not holding to fixed views,
The pure-hearted one, having clarity of vision,
Being freed from all sense desires,
Is not born again into this world (The Metta Sutta).

Important Dates

566 BCE	Siddhartha Gautama born in Lumbini, in what is now Nepal
537 BCE	Siddhartha leaves Kapilavatthu to begin his search for the answer to suffering
531 BCE	On the full moon of May outside the town of Bodhgaya, Buddha attains enlightenment; several weeks later, Buddha delivers his first sermon at Deer Park near Sarnath
486 BCE	The Buddha dies at Kushinagara, aged 80; Kashyapa calls first council, to collect the monastic rules and Buddha's sermons
386 BCE	Second council meets at Vaishali; a major split occurs between traditionalists and liberals
244 BCE	Third council is held at Pataliputra
1st Cent. BCE	A council is held in Aloka Cave, Sri Lanka; monastic rules and sutras are recorded on palm leaves
67 CE	Sutra of 42 Sections is the first sutra to reach China
100 CE	A council of monks meets in Kashmir; rules and sutras were supposedly recorded on copper plates in Greek, but were since lost
4th Cent. CE	Two Indian brothers develop the Yogachara school of Buddhism; Buddhism is introduced into Korea
520 CE	The Indian monk Bodhidharma brings what would become Zen Buddhism to China
538 CE	A Korean delegation brings the first Sutras to Japan
9th Cent. CE	Guru Rinpoche brings Buddhism to Tibet
868 CE	The first printed book—a copy of the Diamond Sutra—is produced in China

Notable Buddhist Holy Days

Southern Buddhists celebrate what is known as Wesak in Sri Lanka and Wisakha in Thailand, on the full moon of May. It commemorates the birth, the enlightenment, and the death of Buddha, which are all believed to have occurred at this time.

Tibetans celebrate Buddha's birth on the 9th day of the 4th month of the old Tibetan calendar. They celebrate his enlightenment and his death on the 15th day of the 4th month.

In Japan, Buddha's birth is celebrated on Hana Matsuri, April 8. His enlightenment is celebrated on February 15 (Nehan). And his death is celebrated December 8 (Rohatsu). Many westernern Buddhists celebrate Buddha Day (Wesak) on the full moon of May.

References and Resources

There are thousands of sutras, and everyone has an opinion on which are most important or most likely the actual words of the Buddha. We have to keep in mind that "authorship" is a fairly modern concept. Buddhist writers often sought to give honor to the Buddha, and practice selflessness, by attributing all their work to Buddha.

The sutras that are most likely actual quotes of the historical Buddha, or at least derived from his earliest disciples, are contained in the Tripitaka (Tipitaka in Pali) or "Three Baskets." There are several versions of this collection, but perhaps the most respected is the one that derives from the texts first recorded in Sri Lanka in the first century, BCE, in the Pali language.

These sutras are available online through the generosity of the southern (Theravada) Buddhist community at a web site called Access to Insight, at http://world.std.com/~metta/index.html. Most of the quotes above are from this site. Among these sutras is perhaps the most beloved book in Buddhism, the Dhammapada. There are also sutras that fall outside the Tripitaka. The best known are the massive Lotus Sutra, the Diamond Sutra, and the Heart Sutra. These are often considered Mahayana (northern) Buddhist texts. It is likely that these are the works of later followers of the Buddhist path, but they are highly significant to northern (Mahayana) Buddhists.

In addition, there are "non-canonical" texts such as the Jataka Tales. These are teaching stories that recount Buddha's former lives. They remind me of Aesop's fables, and can be quite moving. And there are endless texts, ancient and modern, that express Buddha's teachings in prose or poetry, from a variety of cultural perspectives.

For a large online collection, see Washington University of St. Louis' site at http://wuarchive.wustl.edu/doc/coombspapers/otherarchives/electronic-buddhist-archives/. Also see the CyberSangha files at http://worldtrans.org/ CyberSangha/csindex.html. Print texts of the sutras are published by (among others) the Pariyatti Book Service, Seattle, and Wisdom Publications, Boston. Their web sites are at http://www.pariyatti.com and http://www.wisdompubs.org/, respectively.

For selections of Buddhist sutras, look for the following resources:
Goddard, D. ed. 1934. *The Buddhist Bible*. Santa Barbara, CA: J. F. Rowny Press.
Walpola R. 1974. *What the Buddha Taught*. New York: Grove Press.
Suzuki, D. T. 1960. *Manual of Zen Buddhism*. New York: Grove Press.
Thurman, R. 1996. *Essential Tibetan Buddhism*. San Francisco: Harper.

For explanations and interpretations of Buddhist teachings, try these:

Batchelor, S. 1997. *Buddhism Without Beliefs*. New York: Riverhead. A wonderful effort at fitting Buddhism together with Western society (not an easy task!).
Dalai Lama. 1998. *The Art of Happiness: A Handbook for Living*. New York: Riverhead. Written by the leader of the world's Tibetan Buddhists.
Hanh, T. 1976. *The Miracle of Mindfulness*. Boston: Beacon Press. The world renowned Vietnamese monk introduces engaged Buddhism.
Mizuno, K. 1980. *The Beginnings of Buddhism*. Tokyo: Kosei. Buddhism explained within a narrative of Buddha's life.
Snelling, J. 1991. *The Buddhist Handbook*. Rochester, VT: Inner Traditions International.
Suzuki, S. 1973. *Zen Mind, Beginner's Mind*. New York: Weatherhill. In my humble opinion, the very best book ever written on Zen.
The Encyclopedia of Eastern Philosophy and Religion. 1994. Boston: Shambhala. Every Buddhist, Hindu, and Taoist word and name in Sanskrit, Pali, Chinese, and Japanese you are ever going to come across.

NOTES

Courtesy of C. Steven Short

LEO F. BUSCAGLIA
(1924-1998)

By C. Steven Short

Buscaglia was teaching in the Department of Special Education at the University of Southern California in the late 1960s when one of his students committed suicide. She had been one of the sets of "kind eyeballs" he always looked for in the large auditorium, because her responses indicated that at least one student was hearing what he said. The news that she killed herself troubled him greatly. He would lament, "What are we doing stuffing facts into people and forgetting that they are human beings?" Her death prompted him to develop a non-credit class, which he called Love 1A. An ungraded course, Love 1A consisted of lecture and discussion about friendship, love, and the meaning of life. Leo's notes from the class were compiled into a manuscript, which found its way to a publisher's desk. Both author and publisher were surprised to find that the title Love had never previously been claimed for a book. Leo would humorously say, "I have the copyright on Love!" Buscaglia said he never taught Love 1A, only facilitated it. An employee from a local Public Broadcasting System affiliate had heard of his lectures and arranged to record it. The response to the broadcast was so strong that it was forwarded to the national office, which initially considered a professor standing at a podium lecturing outdated and old-fashioned, an anachronism from the early days of "educational television." Still, Leo's message and delivery were so compelling that PBS gave it a try. Years later, critics began to hail Leo as the "granddaddy of TV motivational speakers."

His message of love delivered in his inimitably dynamic style made him a popular guest on television talk shows, as well as on the lecture circuit. At one time five of his books were on The New York Times Best Sellers list simultaneously.

Life is our greatest possession and love its greatest affirmation (Buscaglia, 1982a).

A Cheerleader for Life

Leo Buscaglia was a cheerleader for life. "Life is a banquet," he would say, quoting from the movie *Auntie Mame*, "and most poor fools are starving to death." He was intensely interested in love and human relationships, and was especially cognizant of the value of a gentle human touch.

Hugging became a trademark at lectures, where thousands of people would stand patiently waiting in line to hug him after a presentation. It was not uncommon for him to give a talk of about one hour, then stay afterwards signing books and hugging for at least twice that long. The tradition of hugging at his personal appearances came about when someone offered him a congratulatory hug following an early speech. After a few spontaneous hugs, a line formed, and soon hugging became the anticipated finale to a Leo Buscaglia event. Leo was determined to connect with every individual who wished to meet him. Should someone be left out because they hadn't pushed to the front? Those would have been people he would have missed experiencing, he would say, and that would have left him a lesser person.

He warned against labels—"Republican," "Jew," "disabled"—as distancing phenomena, yet the media tagged him with the names Dr. Hug and Dr. Love. He never especially liked the terms, because they trivialized his work, but he accepted them with grace. If he had to be called something, these were better than many things he could be called.

Of course, when he began the Love 1A class at the University of Southern California, he was roundly criticized by his fellow professors as being overly "touchy feely" and "irrelevant." Such criticism did not dampen his enthusiasm for the sharing that took place weekly between students, parents, and visitors who would eagerly show up at the gatherings. He was very pleased to have been voted Professor of the Year at the University of Southern

California on two occasions, once while teaching Love 1A, and a second time a decade later.

Students who took his counseling and teaching classes thinking they would earn an "easy A" soon learned that while he was an entertaining instructor, he was also a serious one. First and foremost Leo Buscaglia was an educator, and he ran an intense, stimulating class. He was not above throwing erasers and oranges at sleeping students to garner their attention. Leo (1982a) wrote, "Knowledge comes by way of ignorance, so we ought to be encouraged by what we don't know." If your life is not currently what you want it to be, don't blame your past, and don't blame your parents, "and most of all, don't blame God." That was then, this is now. It will take time and effort, but you can change, you can learn, whether your area of interest is music, carpentry or healthy relationships.

Be the Best "You" Possible

Buscaglia (1982a) encouraged people to avoid getting stuck in routines and to relish their individualism.

> As teachers we must believe in change, must know it is possible, or we wouldn't be teaching—because education is a constant process of change (41). And the wonderful thing is, too, that it doesn't matter where you are in that "you." You're only just beginning, because do you know that no one has ever been able to find a limit to human potential? You are *unlimited* possibilities (132).

He also warned against playing what he called "follow the guru." Teachers, guides or gurus "can only give you alternatives. If you follow someone, you're going to become them. And only they can be what they are" (Buscaglia, 1982a, 258).

Leo advised his followers not to imitate him, because maybe he was a banana, and you were a peach. Try as you may, the absolute best result you could ever hope to attain would be to become a second-rate banana. Peaches are wonderful, but they disappoint everyone—most of all themselves—if they try to pass themselves off as bananas. A peach should focus upon being the sweetest, juiciest, most luscious peach possible. Leo (1982a) wrote, "You are the perfect you, and you are the only perfect you who will pass this way in the history of the world" (101). He emphasized individuality by telling listeners that they were "put on this earth for a reason," so their lives should be dedicated to discovering their uniqueness, developing it, and sharing it with the world.

The study of love brought him to the study of life. "To live in love is to live in life, and to live in life is to live in love." But living cannot be done by sitting passively on the sidelines. He wrote, "It's not enough to have lived. We should determine to live for something. May I suggest that it be creating joy for others, sharing what we have for the betterment of personkind, bringing hope to the lost and love to the lonely." Only you will be able to discover, realize, develop and actualize your uniqueness. And when you do, it's your duty to "give it away."

The Good Life

In *Living, Loving, and Learning* (Buscaglia, 1982a), Leo tells an old story of a monk being chased by a hungry bear. Soon the monk approaches a cliff, and has to jump or be eaten. So he jumps—and manages to grab onto the sturdy root of a bush growing out of the cliff. This is very fortunate for him, because there are alligators below, waiting for him to fall! But his safety is again jeopardized, this time by two gophers that appear from under the cliff. Being gophers, they immediately begin to gnaw at the root. What to do, what to do? With hungry bear above, snapping alligators below, and gophers eating away at his lifeline, the monk looks to one side and sees a wonderfully ripe wild strawberry. He loosens his grip just enough to reach out and pluck it, then he pops it into his mouth and thinks, "How delicious."

At first the monk appears foolish for eating strawberries when his life is in danger, but Leo would contend that such an opportunity for enjoyment should not be missed, particularly if the moment proved to be the monk's last on earth. The moral? Live in the moment.

Biographical Sketch

Born in Los Angeles, Felice Leonardo Buscaglia (he later inverted the initials) was the youngest of four children of Italian immigrants. He was raised Roman Catholic, and was influenced by Buddhism in his adult life. The combination of physically demonstrative love of life learned from his

Mediterranean parents combined with the inner reflection learned from travels and studies in Asia served him well.

His childhood is well known to his listeners and readers; it provided many fable-like stories that he shared throughout his career. Many letters to him would begin, "Dear Leo, I hope I can call you that rather than Dr. Buscaglia because I feel as if I know you, as if we are friends...." When someone would identify themselves as a "fan," Leo would invariably reply, "Don't be a fan. Fans are fickle and will soon drop you for something else. Be a friend. You can count on friends."

When he was a boy, a librarian saw him checking out books, one-by-one, in the order they were cataloged on the shelf. The librarian told Leo that it was not necessary to read every single volume in the library, and suggested that he focus on a particular area of interest. One of his favorite early jobs was at the Los Angeles Public Library, where he enjoyed having easy access to the library's vast holdings.

He served in the U.S. Navy in World War II. The slender young sailor did not see combat, but he certainly saw its aftermath in his duties in the dental section of the military hospital, where he helped reconstruct the shattered faces of wounded soldiers.

Using the benefits of the G. I. Bill, he was able to go to the University of Southern California after the war. His association with USC is somewhat unique in the academic world in that he received his bachelors, masters, and doctorate degrees there and later became a faculty member. During his career, Leo spoke to nurses and sheriffs, teachers and insurance agents, and everyone in between, from Singapore to Helsinki, from Anchorage to Acapulco. He said, "I don't speak to professions, I speak to *people*."

Buscaglia received innumerable accolades, including "keys to the city" and various "Lifetime Achievement Awards." But he never accepted honorary academic degrees, saying he worked hard for his, so did not think it proper to claim additional doctorates for merely giving a speech. At the time, his "old fashioned" presentations on national television were the largest single money makers in the history of public television.

More than eleven million copies of his books had been purchased in the U.S. by the time of his fatal heart attack in 1998. Approximately 24 editions are available throughout the world. He was very pleased and surprised by the strong sales in Italy. He never imagined Italians would need an American to remind them of the importance of food, family, sharing, and love of life, because he had learned these things from his Italian parents. An unauthorized video of a speech he gave to an American automaker found its way to South Africa in the days following apartheid. It had such strong underground sales that a company there contacted him to speak to businesses in the "new South Africa."

Interviewers sometimes asked him why he never married. Leo thought that there were two paths available for making the world a better place. One involves marriage, devotion to your spouse and children. A second path involves devotion to the world at-large. He chose the latter path.

When the Road is Smooth

Buscaglia repeatedly advised us to live in the now. All we have is the moment before us. Don't miss out by reliving past experiences, good or bad. Don't miss the moment by dreaming off into an uncertain future. If the road is smooth, celebrate.

When the Road Gets Rocky

As an educator, Buscaglia believed that anything that can be learned can also be unlearned and re-learned. "We can turn despair into hope, and that's magical. We can wipe away any tears and substitute smiles....There are two forces at work, external and internal. We have very little control over the external forces.... What really matters is the internal force. How do I *respond* to those disasters? Over *that* I have complete control."

Leo used to quote cookbook author and TV personality Julia Childs in a variation on the well-known aphorism, "If life gives you lemons, make lemonade." She said if you are planning a soufflé and it falls during baking, don't tell your guests that the dessert is ruined, and don't let it upset your evening. Instead, just whip it up and serve it as a pudding. The events have not changed; the soufflé did not turn out as you had planned, but you have created something new and wondrous out of the debacle. A rocky road may not mean as much as your reaction to it.

When You Encounter a Dragon in the Middle of the Road

First, Leo would look for a way around the dragon, a natural and non-confrontational reaction. There may be a dragon in the middle of the road, but you are not required to go up and poke it with a stick. You do not even have to get into its line of sight. Acting with caution in a potentially dangerous situation is not cowardice, but a sign of intelligence.

Second, if there were no way to avoid the dragon, Leo would probably try to find something to feed it! Sharing was one of the many aspects of food that appealed to him. No one, dragon included, is as confrontational after a good meal. Third, after feeding the dragon, and getting to know it a little in the process—both being activities that would help defuse the tension—he would look for its good qualities. He would try to comment upon the unique qualities of the dragon, which would not be false praise. Could the dragon be trained to breathe fire on the underbrush that would be scratching his legs on the path ahead? Could he convince it to work for the community rather than against it? Most of all, Leo would embrace the possibilities of having a dragon in his path. Once you get over the initial shock of facing the unexpected, the situation might turn out to be fun and rewarding.

About confronting conflict, Leo (1986) wrote, "We need to understand that the process doesn't end once we solve a problem; there will be more ahead. The positive aspect of this is that in those experiences there also exists great potential for growth" (112). "We can consider possible alternatives. It may be helpful to find what others have done in similar situations. With a list of alternatives in hand, we will feel less trapped and more in a position to decide what is best for us" (147).

The Crux: Leo Buscaglia's Advice for Getting a Life

Inevitably, excerpts from a new book by Buscaglia would show up in several national women's magazines, with teasers on the cover proclaiming "Leo Buscaglia's Ten Secrets to a Happy Relationship" or "Eight Steps to a More Loving Marriage." This sort of by-the-book thinking always annoyed him a little. If solutions to the problems of marriage and relationships were so simple, humans would have been issued operating manuals at birth.

Additionally, Leo was fond of saying, "Never give advice. The wise
don't need it, and fools won't heed it." In that spirit, Leo would frown on any
sort of magically easy "list for living." In the introduction of *Born for Love*,
Leo (1992) admitted that he began his day by listening to the news, which was
almost always depressing. In spite of the epidemic of bad news, "I eat my
breakfast, get dressed, and with renewed determination, secure in my armor
of optimism, I face the world as a lover. I know that this may seem naïve and
perhaps a little simplistic to the cynic, but as far as I can determine, it is the
only sensible decision." In *Born for Love*, Leo (1992) also wrote, "Love is
certainly genetically inscribed, but it needs to be evoked, studied, taught and
practiced if it is to have any real meaning."

In a Nutshell

I like to think that the day you're born you're given the world as
your birthday present. A *gorgeous* box wrapped with *incredible* rib-
bons! And some people don't even bother to open the ribbon, let
alone open the box. And when they open the box they expect to see
only beauty and wonder and ecstasy. They are surprised to find that
life is also pain and despair. It's loneliness and confusion. It's all
part of life. I don't know about you, but I don't want to pass life
by. I want to know every single thing in that box (Buscaglia,
1982a, 169).

The Wisdom of Leo Buscaglia

On Loving
Choosing to be a lover doesn't preclude common sense, nor does it
mean that we check our brains at the door (Buscaglia, 1982a).

On Change
I have learned…that a way will only have reality as it relates to living in the now for…life isn't the goal, it's the voyage, and the only
reality seems to lie in change. But if all things that are, are already
ours, then even change is an illusion, and the way becomes simply
an unfolding, like the opening of a flower, for all things necessary
are already a part of us and to discover it we need but nurture the
flower, be patient and continue to grow (Buscaglia, 1973, xi).

On the Care of the Self

I'd like to relate with you about some of the ways in which I think we can be reinforcing, non-melting, gorgeous, tender, loving human persons. First of all the loving individual has to care about himself. This is number one. I don't mean an ego trip. I'm talking about somebody who really cares about himself, who says, "Everything is filtered through me, and so the greater I am, the more I have to give. The greater knowledge I have, the more I'm going to have to give. The greater understanding I have, the greater is my ability to teach others and to make myself the most fantastic, the most beautiful, the most wondrous, the most tender human being in the world" (Buscaglia, 1972, 8).

On Learning

If I don't have wisdom I can only teach you my ignorance. If I don't have joy, I can only teach you my despair (Buscaglia, 1982a).

On Getting Involved

Life means getting your hands dirty. Life means jumping in the middle of it all! Life means going beyond yourself—into the stars! (Buscaglia, 1982a).

On Dignity

Maintain your dignity; maintain your integrity. Nobody can put you down except you (Buscaglia, 1982a).

On Dreams

The greatest dreams that have been accomplished by men and women have once been called impossibilities (Buscaglia, 1982a).

Important Dates

1924	Born in Los Angeles, California
1941	Joined the U. S. Navy
1950	Earned Bachelor's degree in English & Speech
1954	Earned Master's degree in Language & Speech Pathology
1960	Became Supervisor of Special Education, Pasadena (CA) Schools
1963	Earned doctorate in Language & Speech Pathology, with an

	emphasis in the area of stuttering
Mid 1960s	Traveled through Asia, because "it was the part of the world I knew the least about"
1968-1984	Special Education professor in the School of Education, University of Southern California, in Los Angeles
1968	Started Love 1A, non-credit class
1972	*Love* is published
1980	First lecture televised on KVIE-TV, the PBS affiliate in Sacramento, CA
1984	Founded The Felice Foundation, dedicated to "enhancing the spirit of giving"
Mid 1980s	Wrote newspaper column, distributed nationally by *The New York Times* Syndicate
1965-1996	Popular lecturer, speaking to mass audiences throughout the U.S.
1998	Died at his home

References and Resources

Buscaglia, L. 1972. *Love*. Thorofore, NJ: Slack, Inc.

Buscaglia, L. 1973. *The Way of the Bull: A Voyage*. Thorofore, NJ: Slack, Inc.

Buscaglia, L. 1978. *Personhood: The Art of Being Fully Human*. Thorofore, NJ: Slack, Inc.

Buscaglia, L. 1982a. *Living, Loving, and Learning*. Thorofore, NJ: Slack, Inc.

Buscaglia, L. 1982b. *The Fall of Freddie the Leaf*. Thorofore, NJ: Slack, Inc.

Buscaglia, L. 1984. *Loving Each Other: The Challenge of Human Relationships*. Thorofore, NJ: Slack, Inc.

Buscaglia, L. 1986. *Bus 9 to Paradise: A Loving Voyage*. Thorofore, NJ: Slack.

Buscaglia, L. 1987. *Seven Stories of Christmas Love*. Thorofore, NJ: Slack.

Buscaglia, L. 1988. *A Memory for Tino*. Thorofore, NJ: Slack.

Buscaglia, L. 1989. *Papa, My Father: A Celebration for Dads*. Thorofore, NJ: Slack.

Buscaglia, L. 1992. *Born for Love: Reflections on Loving*. Thorofore, NJ: Slack.

Buscaglia, L. 1994a. *The Disabled and Their Parents: A Counseling Challenge* (3rd edition). Thorofore, NJ: Slack.

Buscaglia, L. 1994b. *The Love Cookbook*, (with Biba Caggiano). Thorofore, NJ: Slack.

NOTES

A/P World Wide Photos

JANE GOODALL
(1934-)

By Julie Johnson-Pynn and Tom Pynn

In 1960, a young British woman lacking formal scientific training, but bursting with a love of animals and a dream of roaming the forests of Africa, was commissioned by paleontologist Dr. Louis Leakey to study the wild chimpanzees of Gombe in Tanzania, East Africa. Today, Dr. Jane Goodall is recognized the world over for her astounding discoveries about chimpanzee behavior and her tireless crusade for the well-being of captive and wild populations of animals. "Our understanding of chimpanzee behavior has given us a new perspective on our own position in the scheme of things, has blurred the line, once seen so sharp, between humans and the rest of the animal kingdom. We gain new respect not only for chimpanzees, but also for the other amazing animal beings with which we share the planet. And this urges a new sense of responsibility" (Goodall, 1999a, 11). Jane's courage, tenacity, empathy, and patience, qualities that were cultivated by her observations and reflections of a species "so like us," are shared with audiences on all continents, who delight in hearing her enchanting stories of chimpanzee intelligence, humor, and love.

> Every individual matters. Every individual has a role to play. Every individual makes a difference (Goodall, 1999a, 103).

Forgoing a scientific approach for one of patience and trust, Jane
Goodall entered the lives of the chimpanzees on their terms. Before Jane, the
precedent in the scientific community had been to dub individual animals
with numbers. Instead, Jane referred to her subjects by name—David
Greybeard, Flo, and Passion. Jane wrote an obituary for Flo whom she had
observed for over ten years, the only animal obituary ever published in *The
London Sunday Times*. Her unconventional approach to science, one marked
by an emotional involvement with her subjects, sparked interest in the field of
primatology and helped spur a generation's devotion to conservation.

The Need for Simplicity and Solitude

While many of us succumb to the trappings of Western culture replete
with electric leaf blowers, large screen televisions, and the latest model car,
Jane has always chosen a life without clutter. For someone who regularly
associates with royalty and government dignitaries of many nations, Jane's
house in Dar es Salaam is surprisingly bare. The furnishings include books, a
few photos on the wall, and slips of paper with Swahili translations of English
words for the benefit of the ever-present cadre of volunteers who pass
through. One such sign, "Karibu, You are welcome here," is indicative of her
simple, warm presence.

Her mother Vanne recalls having to insist that Jane purchase new
clothes to replace the shabby ones that were becoming threadbare (Goodall,
1995, 121). At Gombe, Jane would depart for a strenuous day of tracking
chimpanzees with little more than a banana and a handful of raisins. She
writes, "I never feel the need for food, and seldom for water, when I am roaming the forests. How good it felt to be alone at last, reveling in the simple life
that had nourished my spirit for so long" (Goodall, 1999b, 170).

Jane finds solitude to be a necessary component of living. In the quiet
forest she can think deeply about her work, marvel at the majesty of the moon
reflected upon the waves of Lake Tanganyika, and contemplate the days
ahead. "For those who have experienced the joy of being alone with nature,
there is really little need for me to say much more; for those who have not, no
words of mine can ever describe the powerful, almost mystical knowledge of
beauty and eternity that come, suddenly, and all unexpected" (Goodall,
1999b, 72). At Gombe, a large rock edifice jutting out over the forest canopy

has been named "Jane's Peak." It is a sacred place for Jane, an altar where she first offered herself to the chimpanzees, waiting patiently for her subjects to become accustomed to her presence. Years later, after losing her husband Derek to cancer, Jane made a pilgrimage to the peak where she and the chimpanzees sat through a rainstorm together. It was a moment in which she felt the "peace that passeth understanding." Of that experience, Jane writes, "Self was utterly absent: I and the chimpanzees, the earth and trees and air, seemed to merge, to become one with the spirit power of life itself" (Goodall, 1999b, 173). For Jane, the quality of life is enriched by simply *being*. She sees little value in the pursuit of material goods or artificial entertainments.

Striving for Quality of Perception

Although Jane often prefers the solitude of the forest, she recognizes the need to share her perceptions about chimpanzee behavior with the rest of the world. Her observations of chimpanzees using tools and hunting cooperatively helped forge a more complex understanding of primate behavior, and more profoundly, the inextricable ties between mankind and the natural world. In her way, Jane helped redefine what it means to be human.

Jane's careful and unhurried attention to the details of the world enabled her to see, experience, and nurture life's beauty. "We all need, as adults, some experience to make us look at the world again through the eyes of a child" (Goodall, 1999b, 87). As a child, Jane crouched for hours in a chicken coop, waiting for a hen to return so that she could watch it lay an egg—her first exercise as an animal naturalist. At Gombe, Jane watched and recorded the interactions of Flo with her infants. Flo's affectionate and tolerant mothering style resulted in confident and secure youngsters, and Jane used Flo as a model for raising her own child, nicknamed Grub, whose boyhood was spent alongside his mother in the African jungle. Jane never put her career before her son, but instead included him in her naturalist and conservation activities much in the same way that adult chimps include their young in daily activities, showing remarkable patience for their curiosity. Like his mother, Grub has become a significant voice for conservation in Tanzania. Jane urges us to take time to listen to our children's voices so that they may become compassionate citizens.

Upon returning to Gombe from a semester working on her Ph.D. at Cambridge, Jane encountered one of her favorite chimps, David Greybeard, and offered him a red palm nut. "At that moment there was no need of scientific knowledge to understand his communication of reassurance. The soft pressure of his fingers spoke to me not through my intellect but through a more primitive emotional channel..." (Goodall, 1971, 268). The mutuality and reciprocity she experiences with animals is the reason she grieves when one of them dies. Jane points out that "true mourning...can only follow the death of an individual we have known and loved, whose life for awhile has been linked with ours" (Goodall, 1998, 440).

Jane is very sensitive to the interdependence and connections of the life forms surrounding her. For her, the spiritual and the scientific are not mutually exclusive, but should be conceptualized as different windows from which to view the world. Through the panes of Western science we can see "...ever more clearly, into areas which until recently were beyond human knowledge. Through such a scientific window, I had been taught to observe the chimpanzees" (Goodall, 1999b, 175). Through other windows, we can peer at the wonders of life, try to ascertain our individual purpose, or discern the contours of good and evil. When we open up our perspective, we live through our whole being—mind, heart, and soul. The rational mind without the heart and soul too often reduces life to sets of numbers, which limits compassion and narrows the scope of what it means to be human.

Integrity, Humility, and Grace

Unfortunately, since her work has gained worldwide scientific and popular renown, Jane no longer has the luxury of unlimited quiet hours in the forest. Her hectic lecture tours and public appearances dictate that she is in no single place for more than three weeks at a time. How does she maintain the energy to share her wisdom and spread her message of hope while constantly on the move? "Much of it comes from the spiritual power I feel...But an awful lot comes from the amazing people I meet" (Goodall, 1999b, 245). Jane views the people with whom she has shared her life experiences as her teachers and sources of revitalizing energy.

A sense of integrity arises when one grants others respect and approaches people with humility and grace. Just as she relinquishes complete control over the chimpanzees in favor of gaining their trust and cooperation, Jane makes every effort to include the local Tanzanians in her research efforts, asking for their advice and finding them jobs as field research assistants. Helping the community to meet their needs has been an important element in Jane's work since her mother Vanne's pioneering efforts to distribute medical supplies to villagers decades earlier. For example, Jane established a community based project TACARE, the Lake Tanganyika Catchment Reforestation and Education project, that encourages ecologically sound farming and cooking practices, helps educate the populace in health matters, and provides opportunities for responsible economic development.

Consideration of others' perspectives and working to achieve tolerance and compromise are characteristic of Jane's cultural orientation—one that views the world as an intricate, interdependent web of relationships. Friendships between human beings from different cultures begin with understanding and tolerance. When we accept individuals from other cultures on their own terms, we recognize our common bonds rather than superficial differences. Likewise, when we observe the natural world with our hearts, minds, and souls, we gain an understanding of the interconnectedness among all living things.

A Reverence for Life and a Moral Obligation to Serve

Jane has often been criticized for intervening in the lives of her animal subjects. According to some critics, she has not always let nature run its course, provisioning animals with food on some occasions, and on others providing medicine to those who were sick. Rather than blanket all human interactions as detrimental, Jane thinks insightful, careful intervention can yield beneficial results. In *The Chimpanzees of Gombe*, Jane writes "...humans have already interfered to such a major extent, usually in a very negative way...with so many animals in so many places a certain amount of positive interference is desirable" (Goodall 1986, 59).

Jane does not question that animals have consciousness allowing them to feel pain. "Once we accept that a living creature has feelings and suffers pain, and then if we knowingly and deliberately inflict suffering on that creature we are equally guilty. Whether it be human or animal we brutalize ourselves" (Goodall, 1999b, 225). In her books and lectures, Jane describes human-inflicted cruelties on chimpanzees. Jane likens the vacant eyes of chimpanzees behind the steel bars of cages in medical research laboratories to the shocked and hopeless facial expressions of African refugees who fled from neighboring countries into Tanzania. Chimpanzee sanctuaries in many countries of Africa that are directed by The Jane Goodall Institute and are primarily staffed by caring volunteers are the result of Jane's campaign to help these primates.

Acknowledging that in educating children today one is educating the adults of tomorrow, Jane started *Roots & Shoots*, an international humanitarian organization for youth, in February of 1991. Youth who are members of this organization engage in a variety of service activities including tree planting, adopting animals, and cleaning debris from the banks of streams. Jane describes *Roots & Shoots* as "…her most cherished project to date: an international coalition of young people who care about the earth" (Goodall, 1999a, 103). Currently, youth from fifty countries are *Roots & Shoots* members, working together on a mission "…to foster respect and compassion for all living things, to promote understanding of all cultures and beliefs and to inspire each individual to take action and make the world a better place for animals, the environment, and the human community" (www.janegoodall.org/rs/index.html).

The *Roots and Shoots* program is founded upon an ethics that unifies reason and action. Although humans have upset the balance of nature, Jane sees hope in our capacity to solve problems and in our commitment to improving the world. Indeed, the notion that humans are evolving morally as well as biologically is a keystone in Jane's worldview. She writes,

> Only if we understand can we care
> Only if we care can we help
> Only if we help shall all be saved (Goodall, 1999a, 5).

Biographical Sketch

On April 3, 1934, Jane Goodall was born to Mortimer and Vanne Goodall in London, England. After her parents' divorce in 1946, she went to live at the Birches, Jane's mother's family home in Bournemouth. Here, Jane developed the close relationships with living creatures that would become the hallmark of her identity. As a child, she spent most of her time out of doors. In *Reason for Hope* Jane writes, "I loved being outside, playing in the secret places in the garden, learning about nature. My love of living things was encouraged, so that from the very beginning I was able to develop that sense of wonder, of awe, that can lead to spiritual awareness" (Goodall, 1999b, 9). From her early years, a love of great natural beauty led Jane to appreciate the gift of solitude and helped develop her budding spirituality.

As an adolescent, Jane embraced the studies of philosophy, religion, and the composition of poetry. The appointment of Rev. Trevor Davies to her family's church, the Richmond Hill Congregational Church, in 1949 provided the occasion for Jane to rediscover her Christian beliefs. Davies' sermons stimulated her intellectual curiosity and prompted her to read important works in the history of philosophy and to write poetry communicating her understanding of the philosophical and religious ideas she was pondering. He was, she writes, "without a doubt, a major influence in my life" (Goodall, 1999b, 24).

After a trip to Germany in 1953, Jane moved to London and entered a secretarial college. Once there, she also signed up for free evening classes at the London School of Economics. Her coursework included the poetry of Dylan Thomas and T.S. Eliot and an introduction to Theosophy. In the classes on Theosophy, she was exposed to teachings from the east that would influence the development of her worldview: karma, reincarnation, and meditation, what Jane refers to as a way of stopping circling thoughts.

In 1957 after graduating from secretarial college, she went to Africa on the invitation from an old friend. Once in Africa she met Dr. Louis Leakey, and he was so charmed by Jane's enthusiasm and devotion that he took her on as his personal secretary. Three years later Dr. Leakey sent Jane to Tanzania and the Gombe Stream Reserve to set up a research station for observing chimpanzee behavior. It was in the forests of Gombe that Jane would reawaken her love of nature and living creatures and rediscover her deep need for solitude.

On the strength of her work at Gombe and with Dr. Leakey, Jane was admitted as a Ph.D. candidate at Cambridge University in 1962 and graduated with a Ph.D. in Ethology, the study of animal behavior, in 1965. While working on her degree, Jane met and married animal behaviorist and filmmaker Hugo van Lawick. Together they had a son, Hugo Eric Louis (nicknamed Grub), born in 1967. However, Jane and Hugo were divorced in 1974, and in 1975 Jane married Derek Bryceson, a member of the Tanzanian parliament.

Throughout her remarkable life, Jane Goodall has remained firm in her convictions and hope. As she writes in *Reason for Hope*: "My reasons for hope are fourfold: (1) the human brain; (2) the resilience of nature; (3) the energy and enthusiasm that is found or can be kindled among young people worldwide; and (4) the indomitable human spirit" (Goodall, 1999b, 233).

When the Road is Smooth

Help others down the path of life.
In her book, *Walking with the Great Apes*, Sy Montgomery refers to comments made by Geza, one of Jane's field assistants. Geza never imagined as possible the intense bond that he was later to have with one of the Gombe chimps. He marveled that "...Jane had built a bridge strong enough for others to cross" (Montgomery 1991, 118). Jane continues to build bridges, strengthening the ties between people. She carries a stuffed monkey, Mr. H, with her throughout the world. The monkey, which was a gift, has been touched by more than 200,000 people, and Jane tells those who touch Mr. H that the hopeful spirit of the donor will rub off on them.

When the Road is Rocky

Take responsibility for your actions and have faith.
This guiding principle got Jane through "the dark years" at Gombe, when rebels from a nearby country kidnapped some of her researchers. She was ostracized by many in academia for jeopardizing the safety of her students. Yet Jane never doubted that she would find "the strength to get through a day of unhappiness, of suffering, of heartache" (Goodall, 1999b, 11).

When you Encounter a Dragon in the Middle of the Road

View it as an opportunity to cultivate your convictions.
Jane felt weary as a London cab driver began accosting her for wasting money to alleviate the suffering of chimpanzees. His sister also worked for animal welfare. The cab driver argued that the money could be better spent

on humans. Although she was exhausted and not in the mood to defend her position, Jane realized that she was meant to be in that taxi and that she must tell him stories about how remarkable chimpanzees are; how they are so similar to us in many ways. Later, she received a letter from the cab driver's sister who wrote, "something happened to my brother…he's asking me all these questions about animals…he's changed" (Goodall, 1999b, 226-227).

The Crux: Jane Goodall's Ten Crucial Steps to Getting a Life

1. View the world with an open body and mind; be open to possibility.
2. Take risks; challenge yourself.
3. Persevere with both tenacity and patience.
4. Develop your mind, but always remain attentive to your heart.
5. Trust in yourself and others.
6. Share your wisdom and gifts with others.
7. Use your inner strength to bring about positive change.
8. Take time to be alone reflecting on your thoughts and feelings.
9. Be humble.
10. Work for peace in the world and within yourself.

In a Nutshell

Whether human beings and all life emerged as an act of special creation or from evolution is irrelevant to how we live our lives. Human beings have the great capacities of language and intellect which, when informed by compassion, can bring about extraordinary change. Suffering *can* be alleviated; environmental damage *can* be reversed; species extinction *can* be halted and animal populations restored; and, above all, human beings *can* stop destroying one another; human beings *can* love. Every human being has a role to play in this great task.

The Wisdom of Jane Goodall

On the Past and the Future

How humans came to be the way we are is far less important than how we should act now to get out of the mess we have made for ourselves (Goodall, 1999b, 2).

On Responsibility

It's up to *us* to save the world for tomorrow: it's up to you and me (Goodall, 1999b, 251).

On Animal Behavior

The chimpanzees continually surprise us, demonstrating ever more of those qualities that once we believed unique to ourselves (Goodall, 1999b, 152).

On the Power of One

Each one of us matters, has a role to play, and makes a difference. Each one of us must take responsibility for our own lives, and above all, show respect and love for living things around us, especially each other (Goodall, 1999b, 266-267).

On Compassion

If only we could overcome cruelty with compassion we should make a gigantic stride toward achieving our ultimate human potential, moving beyond the Age of Reason to the Age of Love (Goodall, 1999a, 88).

On Religion

With language we can ask, as no other living being, those questions about who we are and why we are here. And this highly developed intellect means, surely, that we have a responsibility toward the other life-forms of our planet whose continued existence is threatened by the thoughtless behavior of our own human species—quite regardless of whether or not we believe in God (Goodall, 1999b, 94).

Important Dates

April 3, 1934	Jane Goodall is born in London, England to Mortimer and Vanne Goodall
1949	Rev. Trevor Davies is appointed to Jane's family's church, the Richmond Hill Congregational Church; he was a significant influence on her spiritual development
1953	Jane moves to London to attend secretarial school
1957	Jane goes to Africa for the first time; meets Dr. Louis Leakey and goes to work for him as his personal secretary
July 16, 1960	Jane begins her work in Gombe Stream Reserve
1963	Jane's first article, "My Life Among the Chimpanzees," is published in *National Geographic* magazine
March 28, 1964	Jane marries Hugo van Lawick
1965	Jane receives her Ph.D. in Ethology, the study of animal behavior, from Cambridge University; (She is the eighth at the university to be awarded the Ph.D. without first receiving her bachelor's degree)
1967	Jane and Hugo's son, Hugo Eric Louis (Grub), is born
1971	Jane's book, *In the Shadow of Man*, is published; goes on to become a best seller
1974	Jane and Hugo divorce
1975	Jane marries her second husband, the Hon. Derek Bryceson, member of the Tanzanian Parliament
May 1975	Rebel guerillas under the leadership of Laurent Kabila kidnap four of Jane's student researchers
1977	The Jane Goodall Institute for Wildlife Research is founded
February 1991	*The Roots and Shoots Program*, empowering youth to make a difference in their community and environment, is founded in Dar es Salaam, Tanzania
1995	Jane is awarded the CBE (Commander of the British Empire) by H.M. Queen Elizabeth II

147

| 1999 | Jane's eighth book, *Reason for Hope: A Spiritual Journey*, is published |
| 2001 | Jane's letters are published as *Africa in My Blood* and *Beyond Innocence*, respectively |

References and Resources

Goodall, J. 1971. *In the Shadow of Man.* New York: Houghton Mifflin Co.
Goodall, J. 1986. *The Chimpanzees of Gombe: Patterns of Behavior.* Boston: Harvard University Press.
Goodall, J. 1999a. *Jane Goodall: Forty Years at Gombe.* New York: Stewart, Tabori, & Chang.
Goodall, J. 1999b. *Reason for Hope: A Spiritual Journey.* New York: Warner Books, Inc.
Goodall, J. 2000. *Through a Window: My Thirty Years with the Chimpanzees of Gombe.* New York: Houghton Mifflin Co.
Miller, P. 1995. "Jane Goodall." *National Geographic Magazine*, 188(3): 102-129.
Montgomery, S. 1998. *Walking with the Great Apes*: Jane Goodall, Dian Fossey, Birute Galdikas. New York: Houghton Mifflin Co.

Adult Books by Jane Goodall

Beyond Innocence: An Autobiography in Letters: The Later Years. (Dale Peterson, ed.). New York: Houghton Mifflin Co., 2001.
Africa in my Blood: An Autobiography in Letters: The Early Years, 1934-1966. New York: Houghton Mifflin Co., 2001.
Visions of Caliban: On Chimpanzees and People. (with Dale Peterson). New York: Houghton Mifflin Co., 1993.

Children's Books by Jane Goodall

The Chimpanzees and Me. 2001. New York: Scholastic, Inc.

The Eagle and the Wren. 2000. New York: North-South Books, Inc.

Jane: The Chimpanzee Family Book. 1997. New York: North-South Books, Inc.

Jane Goodall Websites

www.janegoodall.org The official website of the Jane Goodall Institute.
www.biosci.cbs.umn.edu/chimp/ The Jane Goodall Institute's Center for Primate Studies.

NOTES

Courtesy of David Stephenson

TENZIN GYATSO THE 14TH DALAI LAMA

(1935-)

By Jim Apple

Born in Amdo, Tibet in 1935, Tenzin Gyatso was recognized as the fourteenth incarnation in the line of Dalai Lamas. He became the spiritual leader of Tibet in 1950, at fifteen years old. His tireless efforts on behalf of human rights, nonviolence, and world peace have brought him international recognition. He has lived in exile in India since 1959, when China invaded Tibet. While leading the Tibetan government in exile in Dharamsala, India, he has worked to establish educational, cultural, and religious institutions to preserve Tibetan religion, language, and culture. In 1989, he was awarded the Nobel Peace Prize for his efforts to find a peaceful solution to Tibet's quest for independence. Among Tibetans he is referred to as the Wishfulfilling Gem or simply Kundun—The Presence—epithets that are emblematic of his unique qualities and his special relationship to the Tibetan people.

For as long as space endures, for as long as living beings remain,
until then, may I too abide, and dispel the miseries of the world.

The Dalai Lama's Philosophy of Life

The Dalai Lama's philosophy of life is based on the simple yet profound principle that every human being has the right to happiness. The kind of happiness advocated by the Dalai Lama is one that is "genuine" and long-lasting. Such happiness develops in conjunction with the gradual cultivation of inner peace through ethical restraint and the cultivation of universal compassion.

Underlying Buddhist Principles

The Dalai Lama's philosophy of life comes from the Middle Way school of Universalist Buddhist thought. The formative concepts of this worldview are the principles of universal compassion, cultivation of an altruistic intention to benefit others, dependent origination, emptiness or the lack of essence in persons and things, and every being having the potential to achieve complete awakening.

Among the formative elements in the Dalai Lama's philosophy, the theory of emptiness suggests that all things and events come into being only by means of a process of dependent origination. That is, every living thing is dependent upon other living things; our lives are interdependent and interrelated.

Along with the cultivation of the profound philosophical insight of emptiness, the development of altruism lies at the heart of the Dalai Lama's Buddhist philosophy. Altruism is a selfless motive born of a great compassion towards all things living. "Great compassion" is the spontaneous wish to free others of suffering. One who is capable of dedicating his or her entire being for others is called a bodhisattva. The Dalai Lama is considered to be an advanced bodhisattva.

The ideal figure of the bodhisattva permeates Tibetan Buddhist spirituality and philosophy, including even the myths related to the origins of the Tibetan people. A Bodhisattva transforms his/her altruistic intention for enlightenment into action through the practice of the six perfections. These are:

1. perfection of generosity,
2. perfection of ethical discipline,
3. perfection of patience,
4. perfection of diligence,
5. perfection of concentration, and
6. perfection of discernment.

These six practices are virtues possessed by bodhisattvas like the Dalai Lama as they journey towards Buddhahood.

The Dalai Lama's Advice for Living

Rather than promoting Buddhism as the "best" religion, the Dalai Lama has a supremely tolerant view of other religious traditions. He argues that one should look at the purpose of religions—the promotion of love and compassion for the benefit of living beings—rather than get lost in the doctrinal details. He actively celebrates the diversity that different faiths provide and emphasizes that living a good life is more important than merely talking about it.

The Dalai Lama describes the quintessential quality of religion as compassion, and sees the religions of the world as being concerned with making the mind more peaceful, disciplined, and ethical. From this perspective, all religious traditions have the purpose of aiming for the goal of an enduring happiness, founded upon basic human values. All the world's different religious traditions have the potential to develop warm hearted, good-natured human beings, who practice love, compassion, self-discipline, honesty, and justice.

The Dalai Lama has observed that religions help serve the emotional, mental, and spiritual dispositions that need to be served throughout the world. Just as medicines are available for various conditions of disease, humans need a variety of religious traditions to help heal the spiritual illnesses of hatred, pride, egotism, and jealousy. As the Dalai Lama sees it, humans need a variety of different religious traditions because we are not all plagued by the same vices and weaknesses.

Although he admits that doctrinal differences among religions may seem vast, the Dalai Lama suggests that to make too much of these differences will unnecessarily draw attention away from the common beneficial purpose that religious traditions provide—compassion and love. Religious teachings should not serve as ends in themselves, but should derive their value in providing a framework for living and service to humanity.

Thus, the Dalai Lama (1999a) addresses the problems of modern society from a spiritual, rather than religious, perspective. "I am concerned to try to find a way to serve all humanity without appealing to religious faith" (p.19). Religion is concerned with faith in the claims of salvation and is predicated upon the acceptance of metaphysical concepts (such as heaven and hell) as real. Spirituality is concerned with the qualities of the human spirit that bring happiness to oneself and others—qualities such as love, patience, tolerance, forgiveness, and a sense of responsibility.

According to the Dalai Lama, happiness means "long-term happiness"—"genuine happiness" (1999a, 54-55)—inner peace (1998, 16). The purpose of existence is to seek happiness (1998, 20, 36), a stable and persistent contentment that endures the fluctuations of life's ups and downs, a frame of mind that becomes part of the matrix of our being (1998, 37). The Dalai Lama points out that you do not need more money; you do not need greater fame; you do not need the perfect body or even the perfect mate. He says that right now, at this very moment, you have a mind, and the mind is all we need to achieve complete happiness (1998, 22).

In the Dalai Lama's philosophy, happiness is attained through identifying negative and afflictive mental states and replacing them with positive and wholesome mental states. Material possessions do not necessarily cause unhappiness. Rather, the problem with materialism is the false assumption that satisfaction can arise from gratifying the senses alone. Unlike animals, human beings have the potential to experience a deeper level of happiness that goes beyond the mere gratification of sensory desires (1999a, 25). External factors such as good health, friends, freedom, and propriety are important in establishing well-being, but without inner peace they are not sufficient conditions for genuine happiness.

When you become rooted in concern for others and exhibit sensitivity to the interdependence of the universe, then happiness becomes possible.

> Leaving aside the perspective of spiritual practice, even in worldly terms, in terms of our enjoying a happy day-to-day existence, the greater the level of calmness of our mind, the greater our peace of mind, the greater our ability to enjoy a happy and joyful life (1998, 25).

Although the Dalai Lama emphasizes that human nature is fundamentally gentle and compassionate, he stresses that you must develop an appreciation and awareness of it. Compassion comes about through learning and understanding, and changing how you perceive others and yourself. This developed understanding has an impact on how you interact with others and how you conduct your daily life. The more sophisticated your level of education and awareness about the actions that lead to happiness and the causes of suffering, the more effective you will be in achieving true happiness.

Developing an awareness of mental states is not simply to become more clever, but to bring about discipline within the mind, so that you may engage in more wholesome actions, and cultivate a good heart (1998, 48-49). The qualities of a good heart—love, kindness, and self-confidence—must be developed concurrently with the intellect to achieve the ideal balance.

You transform your innate capacity for empathy into genuine compassion through guarding against factors that obstruct it and cultivating traits conducive to it. That is, you must learn to become aware of unhealthy mental states such as hatred, jealousy, and anger and then consciously replace these emotions with a positive, empathetic concern for others.

In the context of the Dalai Lama's worldview, happiness does not occur out of the blue. Rather, there is a strict correspondence between the cause and effect of your actions based on the Buddhist principle of karma (the causes and conditions of past actions lead to either future suffering or happiness) (1999a, 35-48). Remember, the theory of dependent origination asserts that all living things are mutually dependent upon each other. So, all of your actions, words, and thoughts have implications not only for you, but also for the universe. To achieve happiness, you begin by identifying what makes you happy and what leads to suffering. Then, you gradually eliminate what leads to suffering and cultivate what leads to happiness (1998, 15).

Biographical Sketch

The Dalai Lama, named Lhamo Thondup, was born on July 6, 1935, to a poor family in the village of Takser ("Roaring Tiger") in the province of Amdo. The name, Lhamo Thondup, literally means "Wish-Fulfilling Goddess." The Dalai Lama ("dalai" Mongolian for "ocean" and "lama" Tibetan for "teacher"—"oceanic teacher") is held to be the reincarnation of each of the previous thirteen Dalai Lamas of Tibet (the first having been born in 1391), who are in turn considered to be manifestations of Avalokiteshvara, the Bodhisattva of Compassion.

When Lhamo Thondup was barely three years old, a search party sent out by the Tibetan government to find the new incarnation of the Dalai Lama arrived at Kumbum monastery in the Tibetan province of Amdo. Several fore-telling signs had led the search party there. One of these concerned the embalmed body of Thupten Gyatso, the Thirteenth Dalai Lama, who had died at the age of fifty-seven in 1933. While sitting in state, the head was discov-ered to have turned from facing south to northeast. Shortly after that, the appointed Regent, Radeng Tulku, had a series of visions while meditating upon the waters of the sacred oracle lake, Lhamoi Lhatso, in southern Tibet. Firstly, the Tibetan letters *Ah*, *Ka* and *Ma* came into view within the waters of the lake. Then came the image of a three-storied monastery with a turquoise and gold roof, as well as a path running from it to a nearby hill. Finally the image of a small house appeared. It had unique gutters, and gnarled miniature junipers growing around it.

It was thought that the letter "*Ah*" in the lake referred to Amdo, the province to the far northeast of Tibet. The letter "*Ka*" was thought to refer to Kumbum, the largest and most sacred monastery in Amdo, for it had three sto-ries and a turquoise roof. Finally, the small house in the Regent's vision was thought to be the dwelling in which the Thirteenth Dalai Lama had taken rebirth. In this way, the search party was sent and eventually found the four-teenth Dalai Lama in the Amdo village of Takser.

During the winter of 1940, Lhamo Thondup was taken to the Potala Palace, where he was officially installed as the Dalai Lama, the spiritual leader of Tibet. In the Potala Palace, His Holiness began to receive his pri-mary education. The curriculum was the same as that for all monks pursuing a doctorate in Buddhist studies. The topics for study included Tibetan art and culture, Sanskrit, medicine and Buddhist philosophy. The latter was the most important and difficult part of his studies and consisted of five categories: the perfection of wisdom; the philosophy of the Middle Way; monastic disci-pline; metaphysics; and logic and epistemology.

On November 17, 1950, His Holiness was called upon to assume full political power as head of the State and Government after some 80,000 Peoples Liberation Army soldiers invaded Tibet. At the age of fifteen, the Dalai Lama was enthroned as the leader of Tibet, and found himself the undisputed leader of six million people facing the threat of a full-scale war. In 1954, he went to Beijing to talk peace with Mao Tse-tung and other Chinese leaders, including Chou En-lai and Deng Xiaoping. In 1956, while visiting India to attend the 2500th Buddha Jayanti Anniversary, he had a series of meetings with Prime Minister Nehru about deteriorating conditions in Tibet.

On March 10, 1959, the capital of Tibet, Lhasa, exploded with the largest demonstration in Tibetan history, calling on China to leave Tibet and reaffirming Tibet's independence. The Tibetan National Uprising was brutally crushed by the Chinese army. The Dalai Lama escaped to India where he was given political asylum. Some 80,000 Tibetan refugees followed His Holiness into exile. Today, there are more than 120,000 Tibetans in exile. Since 1960, he has resided in Dharamsala, India, the seat of the Tibetan Government-in-exile.

In the early years of exile, the Dalai Lama appealed to the United Nations on the question of Tibet, resulting in three resolutions adopted by the General Assembly in 1959, 1961, and 1965, calling on China to respect the human rights of Tibetans and their desire for self-determination. With the newly constituted Tibetan Government-in-exile, His Holiness oversaw the immediate and urgent task of saving both Tibetan exiles and their unique culture. Tibetan refugees were resettled and rehabilitated and a Tibetan educational system that raised refugee children with full knowledge of their language, history, religion, and culture was created. The Tibetan Institute of Performing Arts was established in 1959, while the Central Institute of Higher Tibetan Studies became a university for Tibetans in India. More than 200 Tibetan Buddhist monasteries have been re-established to preserve the vast corpus of Tibetan Buddhist teachings, the essence of the Tibetan way of life.

In Washington, D.C., at the Congressional Human Rights Caucus in 1987, the Dalai Lama proposed a Five-Point Peace Plan as a first step toward resolving the future status of Tibet. The plan calls for (a) the transformation of the whole of Tibet into a zone of peace; (b) abandonment of China's population transfer of ethnic Chinese into Tibet; (c) respect for the Tibetan people's fundamental human rights and democratic freedoms; (d) restoration and protection of Tibet's natural environment; (e) commencement of earnest negotiations on the future status of Tibet and of relations between the Tibetan and Chinese peoples.

On December 10, 1989, the Dalai Lama accepted the Nobel Peace Prize on behalf of those who are oppressed and all those who struggle for freedom and work for world peace and the people of Tibet. In his remarks he said, "The prize reaffirms our conviction that with truth, courage and determination as our weapons, Tibet will be liberated. Our struggle must remain nonviolent and free of hatred."

Today, His Holiness the Dalai Lama lives the life of a Buddhist monk in a small cottage in Dharamsala, India. His daily schedule involves rising at 3:00 a.m. for meditation, pursuing an ongoing schedule of administrative meetings and private audiences and giving numerous teachings on Buddhism. He concludes each day with prayers and a meditation. Despite his world acclaim and recognition, along with the passionate devotion displayed by thousands of Tibetans, the Dalai Lama often says, "I am just a simple Buddhist monk—no more, nor less."

When the Road is Smooth

When life is harmonious, reflect upon and rejoice in the causes of happiness. It is important to cultivate a balanced sense of self-worth and fulfillment through rejoicing in the virtuous qualities you have developed.

When the Road Gets Rocky

If there is a solution to the problem, there is no need to worry. If there is no solution, there is no sense in worrying either (1998, 272).

When You Encounter a Dragon in the Middle of the Road

Directly face and confront the dragon. Rather than avoid him, spend some time reflecting on the best way to be of use. Adopt an attitude of tolerance, counteract feelings of anxiety and fear, bring a warm smile filled with empathetic concern, and with a calm and peaceful mind, humbly take on the responsibility for the welfare of both you and the dragon.

The Crux

We cannot escape the necessity of love and compassion. This is my true religion, my simple faith… [i]n this sense, there is no need for temple or church, for mosque or synagogue, no need for complicated philosophy, doctrine, or dogma. Our own heart, our own mind, is the temple. The doctrine is compassion. Love for others and respect for their rights and dignity, no matter who or what they are: ultimately these are all we need (1999b, 234).

Make the rest of your life as meaningful as possible. Do this by engaging in spiritual practice if you can… [i]t consists in nothing more than acting out of concern for others. Relinquish your envy, let go your desire to triumph over others. Instead, try to benefit them. With kindness, with courage, and confidence that in doing so you are sure to meet with success, welcome others with a smile. Be straightforward. Treat everyone as if they were a close friend (1999b, 236).

In a Nutshell

May I become at all times, both now and forever
A protector for those without protection
A guide for those who have lost their way
A ship for those with oceans to cross
A bridge for those with rivers to cross
A sanctuary for those in danger,
A lamp for those without light
A place of refuge for those who seek shelter
And a servant to all in need (1999a, 237).

The Wisdom of The Dalai Lama

On Humanity

The realization that we are all basically the same human beings, who seek happiness and try to avoid suffering, is very helpful in developing a sense of brotherhood and sisterhood, a warm feeling of love and compassion for others. This, in turn, is essential if we are to survive in this ever-shrinking world we live in. For if we each selfishly pursue only what we believe to be in our own interest, without caring about the needs of others, we not only may end up harming others but also ourselves. This fact has become very clear during the course of this century. We know that to wage a nuclear war today, for example, would be a form of suicide; or that by polluting the air or the oceans, in order to achieve some short-term benefit, we are destroying the very basis for our survival (Nobel Lecture, 1989).

On Government

No system of government is perfect, but democracy is closest to our essential human nature; it is also the only stable foundation upon which a just and free global political structure can be built. So it is in all our interests that those of us who already enjoy democracy should actively support everybody's right to do so. We all want to live a good life, but that does not mean just having good food, clothes, and shelter. These are not sufficient. We need a good motivation: compassion, without dogmatism, without complicated philosophy, just understanding that others are our human brothers and sisters and respecting their rights and human dignity. That we humans can help each other is one of our unique human capacities (Forum 2000 Conference, Prague, 1997).

On Happiness

I believe that the very purpose of life is to be happy. From the very core of our being, we desire contentment. In my own limited experience I have found that the more we care for the happiness of others, the greater is our own sense of well-being. Cultivating a close, warmhearted feeling for others automatically puts the mind at ease. It helps remove whatever fears or insecurities we may have and gives us the strength to cope with any obstacles we encounter. It is the principal source of success in life. Since we are not solely material creatures, it is a mistake to place all our hopes for happiness on external development alone. The key is to develop inner peace (Forum 2000 Conference, Prague, 1997).

On Money

Let me say this: money is good. It is important. Without money, daily survival—not to mention further development—is impossible. So we are not even questioning its importance. At the same time, it is wrong to consider money a god or a substance endowed with some power of its own. To think that money is everything, and that just by having lots of it all our problems will be solved is a serious mistake (1999b, 5).

On Responsibility

Whether we like it or not, we have all been born on this earth as part of one great family. Rich or poor, educated or uneducated, belonging to one nation, religion, ideology, or another, ultimately each of us is just a human being like everyone else. We all desire happiness and do not want suffering. Furthermore, each of us has the same right to pursue happiness and avoid suffering. When you recognize that all beings are equal in this respect, you automatically feel empathy and closeness for them. Out of this, in turn, comes a genuine sense of universal responsibility; the wish to actively help others overcome their problems (Universal Responsibility and Our Global Environment).

On the Power of One

I think we can say that, because of the lessons we have begun to learn [from the past], the next century will be friendlier, more harmonious, and less harmful. Compassion, the seed of peace, will be able to flourish. I am very hopeful. At the same time, I believe that every individual has a responsibility to help guide our global family in the right direction. Good wishes alone are not enough; we have to assume responsibility. Large human movements spring from individual human initiatives. If you feel that you cannot have much of an effect, the next person may also become discouraged and a great opportunity will have been lost. On the other hand, each of us can inspire others simply by working to develop our own altruistic motivation (1999b, 161).

On Death

At the time of death, the best parting gift is peace of mind. Knowing this can provide health professionals with a wider perspective on death. They must be open to the fact that people depend on them at this very special moment of their lives, so they should act with a greater sense of responsibility and compassion. It can make a difference. Helping people at the moments of birth and death is one of the most valuable services we can render to humanity (1999b, 106).

On Old Age

The more we reflect on old age and death, the more we see it as a natural process. It is nothing extraordinary. If we prepare ourselves in this way, then when such events actually happen, the work of accepting them as a very normal part of our life is already done. We can simply think, "Now the period where my life ends is coming" (1999b, 107).

On War

Although war has always been part of human history, in ancient times there were winners and losers. If another global conflict were to occur now, there would be no winners at all. Realizing this danger, steps are being taken to eliminate weapons of mass destruction. Nonetheless, in a volatile world, the risk remains as long as even a handful of these weapons continue to exist. Nuclear destruction is instant, total and irreversible. Like our neglect and abuse of the natural environment, it has the potential to affect the rights, not only of many defenseless people living now in various parts of the world, but also those of future generations. Beautiful words are not enough. Our ultimate goal should be the demilitarization of the entire planet. If it was properly planned and people were educated to understand its advantages I believe it would be quite possible. But, if we are to have the confidence to eliminate physical weapons, to begin with some kind of inner disarmament is necessary. We need to embark on the difficult task of developing love and compassion within ourselves. Compassion is, by nature, peaceful and gentle, but it is also very powerful. Some may dismiss it as impractical and unrealistic, but I believe its practice is the true source of success. It is a sign of true inner strength (Forum 2000 Conference, Prague, 1997).

On the Death Penalty

The death penalty is used in two ways: dissuasive and punitive...It is better to pardon. Not forget, but forgive. The deeds such people did were hateful, negative, worthy of being condemned, but they belong to the past. Ultimately, all people deserve compassion and, when necessary, pardon. Even as a preventive measure, I'm not at all convinced that the death penalty has any value whatsoever. If a young person became a criminal through lack of love and affection, more hatred is not going to make the situation right .... There must be other means ... if putting [someone] in jail destroys all hope of reintegrating him into society, then social work would definitely be a better solution (1999b, 100).

Important Dates

1933   Thupten Gyatso, the Thirteenth Dalai Lama, dies at age fifty-seven.
1935   The 14th Dalai Lama is born July 6, named Lhamo Thondup, in Takser village in the Tibetan province of Amdo. He was enthroned as Dalai Lama five years later.
1949   The People's Liberation Army of China, led by Mao Zedong, announces plans to liberate Tibet from foreign imperialists.
1950   The 14th Dalai Lama, then 15, is called upon to assume full political power (head of the State and Government) after some 80,000 Peoples Liberation Army soldiers invade Tibet, with China claiming Tibet has always been Chinese territory.
1956   After seeking refuge in India, he returns to Tibet when Chinese leaders promise there will be no forced reforms.
1959   He attains the highest academic degree of Gashed Lharampa—roughly equivalent to a Ph.D. with distinction.
1959   The Dalai Lama flees to India, with 80,000 Tibetans following him. The Chinese government clamps down on Tibetan uprisings and imposes a military government. Thousands of Tibetans are executed, imprisoned, and sent to labor camps; destruction of Tibetan monasteries begins.
1963   Promulgates a democratic constitution; based on Buddhist principles and the Universal Declaration of Human Rights, as a model for a future free Tibet.
1979   Visits the United States for the first time.
1987   Proposes a Five-Point Peace Plan during a visit to Washington, D.C.
1989   Wins the Nobel Peace Prize.
2001   Issues statement on 42 years of exile and desire for resolution with China.

References and Resources

Selected works by Tenzin Gyatso, the 14th Dalai Lama:
1990.   *Freedom in Exile: The Autobiography of the Dalai Lama.* New York: HarperCollins.

1995. *The Power of Compassion: A Collection of Lectures by His Holiness the XIV Dalai Lama.* Translated by Geshe Thupten Jinpa. London; San Francisco: Thorsons.

1997. *Healing Anger: The Power of Patience From a Buddhist Perspective.* Translated by Geshe Thupten Jinpa. Ithaca, NY: Snow Lion Publications.

1998. *The Art of Happiness: A Handbook for Living.* New York: Riverhead Books.

1999a. Ethics for the New Millennium. New York: Riverhead Books.

1999b. *Imagine All the People: A Conversation with the Dalai Lama on Money, Politics, and Life As It Could Be.* With Fabien Ouaki in collaboration with Anne Benson. Boston: Wisdom.

2000. *Transforming the Mind: Teachings on Generating Compassion.* Translated by Geshe Thupten Jinpa. Edited by Dominique Side and Geshe Thupten Jinpa. London: Thorsons.

2001. *The Compassionate Life.* Boston: Wisdom.

NOTES

Courtesy of http://www.islam101.com

MUHAMMAD
(570-632 CE)

By Amy Johnson

    Muhammad ibn Abdullah was born in 570 in the city of Mecca in the Arabian Peninsula. Orphaned at a young age, Muhammad was raised by his uncle Abu Talib. He became a merchant and trader who was respected for his honesty and trustworthiness. When Muhammad was forty, he received the first of many revelations from God, conveyed through the angel Gabriel. These revelations were recorded, collected, and organized into the Qur'an, the holy book that forms the basis of the religion of Islam. By the time Muhammad died in 632, Islam had become the main religion of Arabia, the Muslim community was recognized as an important and powerful state, and the world had seen the birth of its third major monotheistic religion.

> There are three things which, when you possess them, make you taste the sweetness of faith. First, to love God and his messenger more than all other beings. Secondly, to love others solely for God's sake. Finally, to detest the thought of lapsing into unbelief as much as the thought of being thrown into Hell.

Note: Quotations in the text come from translations of the hadith (reports on the sayings and actions of the Prophet Muhammad) collection of al-Bukhari. Quotes from the hadith are therefore the words of Muhammad; they should not be confused with quotes from the Qur'an, which are the words of God, transmitted to Muhammad via the angel Gabriel.

Principles to Live By

Muhammad and the revelations given to him by God place an emphasis on belief in God, in the unity of God, and in His prophets. While belief in one God may not seem revolutionary today, for most inhabitants of Arabia at the time, Muhammad's teachings were not only peculiar but potentially dangerous. God (referred to in Islam as *Allah*), the Qur'an teaches, can forgive anything except elevation of other entities to coequal status. As Surah 4:48 states, "God forgives not that aught should be associated with Him....Who so associates with God anything, has indeed forged a mighty sin." This revelation led Muslims to prohibit any representations of God or Muhammad; some interpret it as a ban on all artistic representations of humans. The recognition of God's unity and supremacy is the most important declaration of faith; recognition of Muhammad as God's messenger is also required. As the one supreme being, God requires submission from humans. Yet this type of submission should not be likened to the submission of slaves to their master. Rather, the relationship between God and humanity is a loving, compassionate one. This is illustrated in the following hadith:

> The Messenger of God said, "God says, 'I live up to My servant's expectations. I am with him every time that he mentions Me. If he mentions Me to himself, I mention him to Myself. If he mentions Me in company, I mention him in even better company. If he draws near to Me by a span, I draw near to him by a cubit. If he draws near to Me by a cubit, I draw near to him by a fathom and if he walks towards Me, I quicken my pace towards him.'"

In other words, seek God and God will seek you.

The revelations also provide humans with instructions on how to live a good life. The most basic duties of a Muslim are contained in the "Five Pillars of Islam" (discussed below). In general terms, Muslims are enjoined to treat others as they themselves wish to be treated; to institute justice; to be fair and truthful; to be responsible for their own deeds; to be kind, loving, and respectful to their families; to constantly strive to obey God's commands; to pursue knowledge; to use their blessings to assist others in need; to bring others to Islam; to be good examples for others; and when they make a mistake, to recognize it, repent of it, and change their behavior. Muhammad stressed that God is loving, forgiving, merciful, and compassionate. Though both his sayings and the Qur'an make it clear that evil will be punished, they also make it clear that God wants humans to seek Him and to correct their behavior. Accordingly, a person should never think that it is too late to repent.

Advice on Daily Living

The sayings of Muhammad also provided the Muslim community with practical advice on more mundane subjects like personal hygiene ("Have a bath on Friday before attending communal prayer"), diet ("Eat olive oil and anoint yourselves with it, because it comes from a blessed tree"), etiquette ("If you are invited to a marriage feast, go"), table manners ("Don't cut your meat with a knife. That is what foreigners do. Tear it off with your teeth for it is pleasanter and tastier"), the treatment of animals ("Kindness to any living creature will be rewarded"), sharing ("A meal for two is enough for three, a meal for three is enough for four"), medicine ("Black onion seeds contain a remedy for everything except death"), grooming ("Do contrary to the idolaters: let your beards grow, but trim your moustaches"), and suitable clothing ("The person who wears silk in this world will never wear it in the next").

On God, Religion, and Faith

For Muhammad, belief in God was essential. Even before God sent His first revelation to Muhammad, Muhammad had been pondering the meaning of life and searching for a system of belief that would allow people to live a good and moral life. The revelations provided him (and later Muslims) with this system. By acknowledging the presence of God and the necessity of following his instructions, a person could live a satisfying and rewarding life. Surah 6:102 plainly states the necessity of worship, a theme that is repeated throughout the Qur'an, "That then is God your Lord; there is not God but He, the Creator of all things, so worship Him, for He is Guardian over all things."

Technically, anyone who makes the *shahada*, the Muslim confession of faith (saying "There is no God but God and Muhammad is the Messenger of God")—and means it—has become a Muslim. While the religion requires other actions of its adherents, this is the cornerstone of the faith. Surah 2:2-10 provides an introduction to the faith and to the Qur'an itself. It says,

1. This is the Book wherein there is no doubt, guidance to the Godfearing.
2. Who have faith in the Unseen and perform the ritual prayer, and expend of what we have provided them.
3. Who have faith in what has been sent down on you, and what was sent down before you, and are certain of the Hereafter.
4. Those are upon guidance from their Lord; those are they who will succeed.
5. As for the rejecters, alike is it to them whether you have warned them or not warned them, they do not have faith.
6. God has set a seal on their hearts and hearing, on their eyes a covering. For them is a mighty punishment.
7. Some there are of humankind who say, "We believe in God and the Last Day," and they have not faith.
8. They would trick God and the Faithful; only themselves they trick and are not aware.
9. In their hearts there is sickness, and God has increased their sickness. For them is a painful chastisement, for that they called lies.

    Muhammad's sayings and God's revelation to Muhammad contained in the Qur'an express astonishment that humans are surrounded by evidence of the divine, yet they continue to repudiate and doubt its existence.

    In addition to belief in God, Islam also stresses belief in all God's prophets. Muhammad and the religion of Islam recognized all the prophets of Judaism and Christianity, and considered Jesus to have been one of God's messengers (though not God's son). Prophets, including Muhammad, were sent to humanity to teach them God's will and to warn them of the consequences of disobeying the Lord. If one fulfills God's commands and strives to live a righteous life, one will be rewarded; if one ignores God's commands and pursues one's own desires and ends, one will be punished.

On Study and Work

    Muhammad preached that knowledge was essential for all Muslims. He believed in education, and he believed that the pursuit of knowledge was a service to God. Education at this time and in this place did not necessarily mean formal schooling. Like most in his society at the time, Muhammad was illiterate and remained so until his death. However, he preached that all Muslims should strive to learn and increase their knowledge in whatever way possible. He encouraged memorization of the Qur'an and of the hadith reports. He said, "It is the duty of every Muslim, male and female, to seek knowledge." He also likened the pursuit of knowledge to a holy quest, saying, "The person who goes in search of knowledge is on active service for God until he returns."

Moreover, Muhammad was a firm believer in the value of honest work. Growing up in a trading family, Muhammad began his career as a merchant and trader and even met his first wife on the job. Daytime, said Muhammad, is the time God created for men to earn their livings; with their incomes they support themselves, their wives, their children, and their extended families. But one must be careful in one's economic dealings as well. Usury was forbidden by Islam, debtors were encouraged to make the paying of their debts a top priority, and dishonesty in business dealings was considered shameful.

Muhammad considered self-sufficiency important and taught that goods earned are better than those given to you. Muhammad said, "Rather than beg off people who may or may not give you what you ask for, it is better to take some string and make bundles of firewood to sell so that God may preserve your dignity." Yet at the same time, all believers were urged to be generous. Muhammad said, "Spend generously and do not keep an account; God will keep an account for you." He also told his followers, "Avoid Hell by giving charity, even if it means sharing your last date, and if you have nothing at all, by speaking a kind word." Indeed, asking for help is permitted, and the less fortunate have a right to assistance from those who have been blessed with more goods. There is no shame in asking for assistance when you require it, as the following saying indicates, "The really poor person is not the one whom you send away after giving him a date or two, or one or two mouthfuls of food. The really poor person is the one who does not dare ask."

What is the "Good Life?"

This question was one that Muhammad found easy to answer. The good life, he believed, consisted of striving to follow God's commands in all that one does. The good life was not to be found in the pursuit of wealth, beauty, or physical pleasure. Tempting as those things may be, and there are appropriate outlets for their pursuit and enjoyment, they are not ends in themselves. The good life means believing in God and his prophets, performing daily prayers, fasting during Ramadan, giving to those less fortunate than yourself, and performing the pilgrimage. It means treating others as you would want to be treated. It means respecting your parents, being kind to your spouse, and raising your children in a loving manner. It means refraining from lying and being critical of others who are trying to live correctly (though you should help them in their efforts when you see them stumbling), and not being a hypocrite. It means knowing what you believe in and not being afraid to speak out in defense of your beliefs and against what you see as wrong, even if speaking out may sometimes be risky. This life, Muhammad taught, is essentially a test; only by living correctly in it can one be judged favorably on the day of judgment and thereby gain access to paradise.

On Marriage, Sex, and Family Life

Muhammad's first wife was a wealthy widow who was fifteen years older than he was. The couple met when Khadijah, who knew of Muhammad's reputation as a trustworthy and honest businessman, hired him to look after her economic affairs. She was impressed with the way Muhammad conducted business on her behalf, and she soon proposed to him. The couple had six children, two of whom died in infancy, and lived happily together until Khadijah's death. Khadijah was the first convert to Islam and the one to whom Muhammad first turned to discuss the revelations he received from God. While Khadijah lived, Muhammad did not marry again, despite the prevalence of polygamy in the Arabian Peninsula that predated Islam.

After his beloved wife died in 619 and before his own death in 632, Muhammad married nine other women (a tenth woman was raised to the status of wife after bearing Muhammad's son). While many people today criticize polygamy, it must be remembered that it was once quite acceptable. Muhammad's wives were often widows of converts to Islam who had been killed in battle or women whom he married for political reasons. The exception was his favorite wife, the young Aisha, daughter of his close friend Abu Bakr, one of the earliest converts. Muhammad and Aisha married when Aisha was eleven. Though a young age for marriage by modern standards, marriage at the onset of puberty was not uncommon at the time. Aisha became Muhammad's confidante and favorite wife, and she served as a model for Muslim women. She helped Muhammad spread the message of Islam, went into battle alongside her husband, and even preached to new female converts. However, Muhammad's multiple marriages were a special case; the Qur'an restricts the number of women a man can marry to four and further commands that unless he can treat all his wives equally, a man should marry only one woman. Though Islam does not regard marriage as a sacrament, it is an important social institution, something that both the Qur'an and Muhammad regarded as incumbent upon all believers as long as they are physically and financially able to marry.

Muhammad once said that "When a worshipper of God has taken a wife he has perfected half his religion." Marriage is an important institution for cementing social ties and legitimizing sexual expression. He believed that "Men will always be subject to carnal desires, whether or not they gratify them." Islam, in eschewing monasticism and encouraging marriage helped provide a suitable outlet for physical desire. It also attempted to reduce the temptation of inappropriate sex by encouraging gender segregation, modest dress for both men and women, and relatively early marriage. Muhammad's advice was as follows, "Young people, if you are capable of supporting a family you should marry. If you are not, then fast, because fasting will protect you." The Prophet understood the human desire for sex, and he did not regard it as something shameful. But he did preach that the sexual impulse should only be satisfied within the marriage relationship. Even after marriage, he recognized that a man might feel desire for a woman other than his wife. His advice? "If you fancy a woman and become infatuated with her, go and make love to your wife."

Muhammad's relationship with his wives is often held to be the ideal family relationship. In Islam, both partners in a marriage are seen as equal, but both are endowed with different abilities and hence both are responsible for different tasks. Women are the primary caretakers of the home; their first duty is to raise their children, take care of their husband and family, and look after the religious and moral development of the family. Men, on the other hand, are responsible for the maintenance of the household and for the protection and supervision of the family. Fidelity is required of both marriage partners; sexual intercourse outside the marriage relationship (or, in the early days of Islam, with women who were not captives or slaves of the man) is forbidden. Divorce is permitted, but it is not encouraged; Muhammad is known to have said that "Of all lawful things, the one which God dislikes most is divorce."

Muhammad also emphasized the necessity of treating one's family well. Numerous sayings of the Prophet stress the obligation of believers to treat parents, especially mothers, well. Although some Islamic legal scholars believe a husband is allowed to lightly beat his wife, many of the sayings of Muhammad make it clear that he disapproved of this type of violence. Muhammad preached that men should treat their wives well, provide for their wives and children, listen to and consider their wives' advice and opinions, and be kind to their wives' families. He taught that women should also treat their husbands well, raise their children properly, be kind to their husbands' families, respect their husbands' wishes, be obedient, and be grateful for their husbands' support.

Yet there are numerous sayings of the Prophet that many women today might find offensive. One such saying is that "Isn't the testimony of a woman worth only half the testimony of a man? That is because of her inferior intelligence." Another says, "Women can be as alluring as Satan and will egg you on like Satan." Whether or not one agrees with these sayings, it should be noted that Islam advanced the status of women in Arabia by placing restrictions on polygamy, prohibiting the practice of female infanticide, and giving women numerous legal and property rights they had not been granted before. It is also important to recognize that some newer interpretations of the Qur'an and of the sayings of Muhammad place more emphasis on the equality of all believers regardless of gender and do not condone polygamy (with the exception of the Prophet). These newer interpretations stress a "big picture perspective" of the Qur'an rather than focus upon a verse in isolation.

Biographical Sketch

Muhammad was born in 570 in Mecca in what is now Saudi Arabia. His father died before his birth, and his mother died when Muhammad was a child. Muhammad was raised by his uncle, Abu Talib. His family was not extremely wealthy, but it was an established and well-respected family in

Mecca. The family was part of the Quraysh tribe, the ruling elite of the city. Muhammad grew up to be a trader and merchant and was known throughout Mecca for his honesty and fair dealings; the people of Mecca gave him the nickname *al-Amin* ("the trustworthy") because of his good reputation. At the age of twenty-five, Muhammad was hired to look after the economic interests of a wealthy widow named Khadijah. Although Khadijah was in her forties, the couple soon married and had six children, two boys who died in infancy and four girls. After Khadijah died, Muhammad married several other women, but while she was alive, she remained his only wife.

Muhammad had always tried to live a good, moral life, and when he was in his thirties he began to take a more intense interest in philosophy and religion. He began meditating in a cave in the mountains outside the city, and in the year 610 God sent the first of many revelations to Muhammad. The first revelation occurred when the angel Gabriel appeared to Muhammad and instructed him to read. As Muhammad was illiterate, he was confused by the command, which Gabriel had to repeat several times. Muhammad memorized the revelation, as he did all subsequent ones. These revelations were later recorded, collected, and organized into the Qur'an, the holy book of Islam.

Muhammad initially spoke of his experience only to his wife; Khadijah was the first to believe in the revelations. Other early converts came from Muhammad's family and close friends. After Muhammad was instructed by God to proclaim the revelations publicly, the new Muslim community began to face problems in Mecca. As more people began converting to Islam, the ruling tribe, the Quraysh, began to persecute Muhammad and his followers. They saw the Muslims as a threat to their own position of leadership and their wealth in the city.

This persecution led Muhammad and his followers to emigrate from Mecca to the city of Yathrib in 622. The city of Yathrib was internally divided between the well-established Jewish tribes and the relatively new pagan tribes. The leaders of the city encouraged Muhammad's move to Yathrib because they saw him as a strong, neutral leader who could help heal the city's divisions. From their new base in Yathrib (also known as *al-Medina al-Munawarrah*, The Luminous City, or *Medinat Rasul Allah*, The City of God's Messenger, or *Medinat al-Nabi*, the City of the Prophet, or *Medina*), the Muslims mounted attacks on Quraysh trading caravans from Mecca. After a long series of battles, Mecca was forced to surrender to Muhammad in 630. In 632, Muhammad, his wives, and a group of over 100,000 Muslims performed the pilgrimage to Mecca. During this "Farewell Pilgrimage," Muhammad preached his last sermon on the Plain of Arafat. Shortly thereafter Muhammad died, and leadership of the Muslim community passed to his companions Abu Bakr (632-34), Umar (634-44), Uthman (644-56), and Ali (656-61); following Ali's death, succession disputes caused the Muslim community to split into two sects, later called the Sunnis and Shi'ites.

God's revelations to Muhammad through the angel Gabriel established a new religion. The new religion of Islam (literally meaning "submission") emphasized morality, fulfillment of one's duty, equality of believers, and modesty. Each Muslim (literally, "one who submits," i.e., to God's will), is required by the faith to do five things. These five duties are often called the Five Pillars of Islam. They are *shahada* (saying the confession of faith: "There is no God but God and Muhammad is the Messenger of God"), *salat* (prayer, which is to be performed five times a day while facing the city of Mecca), *sawm* (fasting during the holy month of Ramadan, the ninth month in the Islamic calendar), *zakat* (the giving of alms or charity), and *hajj* (performing the pilgrimage to Mecca in the appointed month at least once in one's lifetime, assuming one is physically and financially able to do so).

This new religion changed the social, political, and religious landscape of the Arabian Peninsula. It helped bring an end to practices such as idol worship and female infanticide in Arabia, and it provided a new basis for communal identity that transcended the old bases of wealth and tribal lineage. It became the guiding ideology of many powerful empires and states (e.g., the Umayyad and Abbasid caliphates, the Mamluk and Delhi Sultanates, the Empire of Mali, the Kingdom of Ghana, and the Ottoman and Mughal Empires). Islam eventually spread to many other areas of the world, including Africa, Asia, and Europe. Today, Islam is the second largest religion in the world in terms of number of believers, and it is the fastest growing religion in North America.

When the Road is Smooth

Recognize that all good things come from God. Do not be arrogant or proud. If you receive great wealth, you have a duty to use it to help others, and they have a right to share in your success. If you receive fame, use it to set a good example for others. If you become known for your knowledge, you have received a great gift from God. Use it for His glory, rather than for your own.

When the Road Gets Rocky

Recognize that problems are temporary but faith is eternal. Do not give up your attempts to live a good and pious life. If you fulfill God's commands you will be rewarded in paradise, even if this life is not always easy. Remember that God is merciful and compassionate. Be aware that as bad as things may seem, there are always people who are suffering more than you are. Help them when you can, and do not be hesitant to ask for help from others yourself. There is no shame in asking for assistance, and those who have much are required to share it with those who have little; indeed, it is the right of the less fortunate to be assisted by those who are more fortunate.

When You Encounter a Dragon in the Middle of the Road

Recognize it as one of God's creations. If it can reason, tell it about God, the revelations, and the message of Muhammad. If it recognizes the beauty of the revelation and the message, you have performed a praiseworthy duty by bringing another creature to Islam. If it refuses to listen, you have fulfilled a duty by warning and instructing it. If it becomes hostile, attempt to get around it. If it attempts to force you to renounce your faith or perform an illicit act, or if it attacks you and you believe your life to be in jeopardy, you are within your rights to strike back. If you have to kill it, you must do so mercifully and quickly, without causing it to suffer.

The Crux: Muhammad's Commandments for Living

1. Believe in God and his Messenger.
2. Obey God's commands and fulfill the "Five Pillars of Islam" (confession of faith, prayer, fasting, charity, and pilgrimage).
3. Treat others as you want to be treated and love others for God's sake.
4. You are responsible to God for your actions; do not waste the gift of life on

trivial things or blame others for your deeds.

5. Pursue knowledge; its pursuit is a means of serving God.
6. True wealth is not found in worldly goods but in the soul.
7. Dress and live modestly.
8. Honor and respect your parents, especially your mother, and treat your family well.
9. Do not succumb to temptation; this world is transitory.
10. It is never too late to mend your ways. God is compassionate, merciful, and forgiving.

In a Nutshell

O you who believe, fear God and believe in His Messenger. He will give you a double portion of his favor and appoint a light for you to walk in; God is All-Forgiving, All-Compassionate (Qur'an 57:29).

The Wisdom of Muhammad*

On Relating to Others
None of you really believes until he desires for his fellow Muslim what he desires for himself (SB 1.10, Anas).

On Good Deeds
Three things follow a dead person to the grave and two of them return while one remains with him. His family, his wealth, and his deeds follow him; his family returns home with his wealth, but his deeds remain (MM 5167, B&M, Anas).

On Avoiding Temptation
Between what is clearly permitted and what is obviously illicit there are doubtful cases. The person who refrains from what he thinks might be sinful will be led to refrain from what is clearly illicit. The person who is inclined to do what he thinks might be sinful will be led to do what is obviously illicit. Sin is God's private pasture; if you graze in its vicinity, you will run the risk of entering it (SB 3.69, an-Nu'man b. Bashir).

On Honest Work

Nobody ever eats a better meal than the one which he has earned with his own hands. God's prophet, David, used to eat what he gained by the work of his own hands (SB 3.74, al-Miqdam).

On Honoring Parents

Abu Hurayra said, "A man came and found the Messenger of God and said to him, "Messenger of God, who has the most right to be well treated by me?" He replied, "Your mother." So the man asked "And then who?" He replied, "Your mother." The man asked, "And then who?" He replied, "Your mother." Again the man said, "And then who?" He replied, "And then your father" (SB 8.2).

On Truth

Truthfulness leads to piety and piety leads to Paradise. A person should always be truthful so as to merit the name Very-truthful. Lying leads to immorality and immorality leads to Hell. Man keeps on lying until he is marked down in God's eyes as an inveterate liar (SB 8.30, 'Abdallah).

On Obedience

Whoever obeys me, obeys God; whoever rebels against me, rebels against God. Whoever obeys my delegate, obeys me; whoever rebels against my delegate, rebels against me (SB 9.77, Abu Hurayra).

On Responsibility

All of you are shepherds responsible for your flocks. A ruler is shepherd of his subjects and he is responsible for them. A man is shepherd of his family and he is responsible for them. A woman is shepherd of her husband's home and she is responsible for it. A servant is shepherd of his master's wealth and he is responsible for it (SB 2.6, 'Abdullah b 'Umar).

quotations are from two hadith collections: SB = Sahih al-Bukhari; MM = Mishkat al-Masabih of Tabrizi.

Important Dates

570 CE   Muhammad born in Mecca to Aminah bint Wahb; his father, Abdullah ibn Abd al-Muttalib dies before Muhammad is born

575 CE	Muhammad's mother dies; Muhammad goes to live with his grandfather, Abd al-Muttalib
578 CE	Muhammad's grandfather dies; Muhammad goes to live with his uncle, Abu Talib
582 CE	Muhammad accompanies his uncle to al-Sham on a trading expedition; a monk at Busra recognizes the signs of prophethood in the boy
585 CE	Muhammad participates in the Fijar War; marks first participation in armed conflict
610 CE	While meditating in the mountains outside Mecca, Muhammad receives his first revelation from God via the angel Gabriel; early converts are family members and close friends; new Muslims worship in secret for three years
613 CE	God tells Muhammad to publicly proclaim Islam; public preaching begins and widespread conversion follows; persecution of Muslims by the elite of Mecca begins, but is tempered by the respect of the Quraysh for Muhammad's uncle, Abu Talib
621 CE	*al-Isra* (the Night Journey) and *al-Miraj* (The Ascension) take place; during one night, Muhammad meets the previous prophets, sees the Angel of Death, goes before the throne of God, and journeys to Jerusalem on Boraq (a creature with a human head, a horse's body, and the wings of an eagle)
622 CE	The *Hijrah* (emigration) takes place; persecution in Mecca leads Muslims to emigrate from Mecca to the city of Yathrib (later called Medina); construction of Prophet's Mosque begins in Yathrib; Muhammad serves the city as a political leader and settler of disputes; Muhammad begins to call for conversion of Jewish population of Yathrib; hostility between two communities begins
628 CE	Treaty of Hudaybiyah between the Quraysh and the Muslims is signed, marking Quraysh recognition of Muhammad as an equal leader and Quraysh acceptance of a Muslim state in Arabia; missions begin to be sent throughout Arabia; Jewish communities forced to submit to Muslim authority
630 CE	Muslim conquest of Mecca; general amnesty for opponents of Muhammad declared

632 CE   Year of Deputations: mass conversions in Arabia as tribes send delegations to Muhammad to declare their conversion and loyalty; non-Muslims barred from performing the pilgrimage to Mecca; Muhammad and his wives and more than 100,000 Muslims make the pilgrimage to Mecca; Muhammad preaches his final sermon on the Plain of Arafat; Muhammad dies.

**Some dates are approximate, and scholars differ on dates of certain events.*

References and Resources

Ali, A.Y. 1946. *The Koran: Text, Translation, and Commentary.* Washington, DC: American International Printing Company.

Armstrong, K. 1992. *Muhammad: A Biography of the Prophet.* San Francisco: Harper.

Denny, F. 1985. *An Introduction to Islam.* New York: Macmillan.

Esposito, J. L. 1998. *Islam: The Straight Path.* Oxford: Oxford University Press.

Graham, W. 1977. *A Divine Word and Prophetic Word in Early Islam.* The Hague and Paris: Mouton.

Haykal, M. H. 1976. *The Life of Muhammad.* (Isma'il Ragi A. al-Faruqi, Trans.). Indianapolis: North American Trust Publications.

Ibn Ishaq. 1967. *The Life of Muhammad.* (Alfred Guillaume, Trans.). London: Oxford University Press.

Khan, M. M. 1979. *The Translation of the Meanings of Sahih al-Bukhari.* Chicago: Kazi Publications.

Peters, F. E. 1994. *Muhammad and the Origins of Islam.* Albany: SUNY Press.

Renard, J. ed. 1998. *Windows on the House of Islam: Muslim Sources of Spirituality and Religious LIfe.* Berkeley: University of California Press.

Robinson, N. ed. and trans. 1998. *The Sayings of Muhammad.* Hopewell NJ: Ecco Press.

Schimmel, A. 1975. *And Muhammad is His Messenger.* Chapel Hill: University of North Carolina Press.

Williams, J. A. 1994. *The Word of Islam.* Austin: University of Texas Press.

NOTES

Courtesy of http://www.umass.edu/wsp/news/kit/gallery/confucius.html

MASTER KONG (CONFUCIUS)
(551-479 BCE)

By David Jones

*Master Kong, or Confucius as he is known in the West, is recognized
as China's first great teacher who exerted widespread influence throughout
Southeast Asia, especially Korea and Japan, and is now gaining attention
from Western thinkers. Kongzi was born in the ancient state of Lu during tur-
bulent times when fourteen independent states were vying for power that
would ultimately lead to the emergence of the imperial Chinese state. Such a
political and military context set the stage for Confucius' thinking about how
to live and die together in meaningful, peaceful, and harmonious ways. The
words from one of the world's most influential thinkers comes down to us
through a collection of sayings referred to commonly as the <u>Analects</u>, which
were compiled by a few of his disciples shortly after his death. In the <u>Analects</u>,
we come to know the vision of this great thinker who influenced more people
across the planet than any other.[1]*

Note: Quoted text comes from *The Analects of Confucius: A Philosophical
Translation* by Roger T. Ames and Henry Rosemont, Jr. (Ballentine Books,
New York 1998).

Authoritative persons establish others in seeking to establish themselves and promote others in seeking to get there themselves.
Correlating one's conduct with those near at hand can be said to be
the method of becoming an authoritative person.

Acknowledging Li

Li are the canons and mores of society that help define us in relation
to the past and assist us in creating the future. Harmonious relations in the
community are considered among the most divine aspects of human existence. This is why when asked about how to serve the spirits and the gods,
Confucius replies, "Not yet being able to serve other people, how would you
be able to serve the spirits?" (11.12).

The focus on humanity is given its expression through *li*, and is
essential to Confucius' perception of what constitutes the good life. As the
Master said, "Do not look at anything that violates the observance of ritual
propriety; do not listen to anything that violates the observance of ritual propriety; do not speak about anything that violates the observance of ritual propriety; do not do anything that violates the observance of ritual propriety"
(12.1).

Confucius advocates cultivating the self through tradition (*li*). In
Western culture, the self is considered a substantial being with an inherent
essence. The Western view suggests the existence of a transcendent God to
which the self appeals for salvation. Thus, the self bestows upon itself an
immortal soul that extends its "life" beyond the life of the body. The "truth"
of this type of thinking is often accepted without challenge and finds its way
into our everyday parlance ("God bless you" after a sneeze), on our money
(In God We Trust), and in our courtrooms (I swear to God). In the Western
intellectual and religious tradition, the self develops through abstract reasoning and may even become an abstraction itself. Society is considered a collection of individuals, each with certain inalienable rights in this life and enti-
tlements in the next.

On the other hand, the Chinese view the self as a composite process
of relations. Society defines the individual—who we are, is an expression of
the context from which we have emerged. Consequently, society serves as a
repository of values, not an arena for actualizing human potential. Individual
rights become secondary to the larger needs of the community. With such a

HOW TO GET A LIFE

focus, we can better understand why most Chinese value collective "rites" or *li*, over individual "rights."

The word *li* has the connotation of a holy ritual or sacred ceremony.[2] This historical dimension is crucial for understanding the philosophy of Confucius because it is through the proper practice of *li* that the self enters the realm of tradition. This participation in tradition has a magical quality, since performing our *li* in the proper spirit will transform us and those around us.

Both the sacred and magical dimensions of *li* ultimately lead to harmony and order. The development of *li* is not consciously driven or ordered by some external and transcendent source such as God, the Platonic Idea of the Good, or even compliance with some abstract moral principle. *Li* emerge from their social context and our communal history and govern the patterns of social intercourse.[3] *Li* are the emerging principles that give coherence to societies that arise from the context of human interactions. *Li* are concrete examples of our humanity, of who we are. If harmony and order are our primary goals, as they are for Confucius, we must affirm the values emerging from our tradition as being sacred. For Confucius, what and who we are in the most profound sense is a product of the authentic tradition that separates us from the nonhuman.

Junzi

If the exemplary person, or *junzi*, acts in accordance with *li*, effects of his/her actions follow in natural ways. If we can incorporate acting in accordance with *li* into our lives at home, in the neighborhood, and in the workplace, we can achieve results that resonate with the *junzi*'s actions. The goodness of the *junzi* is contagious and has an amplifying effect in those he/she encounters. Confucius encourages us to recognize our everyday lives through our *li* and to realize the transformative power of *li*. We can begin to see this transformative power in the responses of those whom we engage through the medium of *li* and use this experience as an entrée into our own transformation. How else could we relate to others, especially those outside our immediate context, without a medium through which we can express our warmth, concern, and compassion?

In the *Analects*, Confucius notes how the *junzi*'s behavior prompts "magical" emulation:

1. The Master said, "Governing with excellence can be compared to being the North Star: the North Star dwells in its place and the multitude of stars pay it tribute" (2.1).
2. The Master said, "Lead the people with administrative injunctions and keep them orderly with penal law, and they will avoid punishments but will be without a sense of shame. Lead them with excellence and keep them orderly through observing ritual propriety and they will develop a sense of shame, and moreover, will order themselves" (2.3).
3. Ji Kangzi asked Confucius about governing effectively, and Confucius replied to him, "Governing effectively is doing what is proper. If you, sir, lead by doing what is proper, who would dare do otherwise?" (12.17).
4. Ji Kangzi asked Confucius about governing effectively, saying, "What if I kill those who have abandoned the way to attract those who are on it?" "If you govern effectively," Confucius replied, "what need is there for killing? If you want to be truly adept, the people will also be adept. The excellence of the exemplary person (*junzi*) is the wind, while that of the petty person is the grass. As the wind blows, the grass is sure to bend" (12.19).

As the *junzi* looks, listens, speaks, and moves in accordance with *li*, others follow his/her example without coercion or force.

Ren

While *li* provide the framework, authoritative conduct, or *ren*, is the spirit that we must bring to *li* to become a *junzi*. *Ren* means to become an authentic human being.[4]

The adage attributed to the Chinese that a picture is worth a thousand words is a good place from which to begin when discussing *ren*. The everyday term *ren* simply means person, but to become a *junzi* one must become *ren*. This second *ren* is the highest Confucian virtue and is written a bit differently from the character for person. This highest virtue of *ren* in Confucian thought is derived by adding the number two (*er*) to *ren* (person).[5] What this picture suggests is that the highest virtue in Confucius' thought is achieved by adding two (persons) to one. In other words, the highest virtue of *ren* (authoritative conduct or authoritative person) is only achievable in relationships of three or more, that is to say, only in relationships that constitute a family or community.

Of course, maintaining harmony among a diverse set of individuals can be a complex task. One cannot become an authoritative person (a *ren* person) "in Descartes' closet" (Hall and Ames, 1998, 259). In other words, one cannot become *ren* or a *junzi* in isolation, even if one proclaims his existence just because he thinks, as Rene Descartes did when he wrote, "I think, therefore I am."

Ren is a kind of conduct that comes with the authority of accomplished individuals such as Michael Jordan in the appropriate context of a basketball game or Tiger Woods on a golf course. Although *ren* also connotes virtue and benevolence, it is clear from the *Analects* that there is nothing easy about its attainment. Students of Confucius constantly ask him whether rulers or contemporary political figures have attained *ren*, but his answer is always no! The attribution of *ren* is only ascribed to figures of China's mythic past. Thus, *ren* becomes a goal as elusive as reaching the horizon. Even when disciples of Confucius entreat him about his own achievement of *ren*, he self-consciously replies: "How would I dare to consider myself a sage or an authoritative person [*ren*]? What can be said about me is simply that I continue my studies without respite and instruct others without growing weary" (7.34). This modest refusal and the ascription of *ren* emphasizes that becoming human is a continual process. *Ren* is not some sort of ultimate achievement where one rests upon his/her laurels or where one has finally achieved an enlightened or forgiven state. To become a *junzi*, a person must never rest or grow complacent.

The Golden Rule According to Confucius

When asked if there is "one expression that can be acted upon until the end of one's days," Confucius replies: "There is *shu*: do not impose on others what you yourself do not want" (15.24). In 12.2, this same point is underscored as Zhonggong inquired about authoritative conduct (*ren*). The Master replied, "In your public life, behave as though you are receiving important visitors; employ the common people as though you are overseeing a great sacrifice. Do not impose upon others what you yourself do not want, and you will not incur personal or political ill will."

In his application of the Golden Rule (which predates Christianity), Confucius emphasizes "not doing" over "doing." When one does unto others what one wishes to be done to her/him, the benefactor of the "doing" is the self. Instead of identifying the self as a beneficiary of rewards for good behavior, Confucius' version of "not-doing" requires constant vigilance, restraint, and discipline. The self is eliminated from the equation. Hence, the *junzi* achieves *ren* through participating in the welfare of her fellow human beings. For Confucius, there is no room for selfish behavior or attitudes of self-indulgence. The *junzi* is not motivated by self-interest or profit.

The Endless Quest

Confucius reinforces the difficulty of becoming *ren* by applying the idea of the *junzi* to himself, "As far as personally succeeding in living the life of the exemplary person (*junzi*), I have accomplished little" (7.33). "What can be said about me is simply that I continue my studies without respite and instruct others without growing weary" (7.34).

According to Confucius, there is no ultimate goal; we need to constantly work through our disciplined practice to become a *ren* person or *junzi*. "Exemplary persons [*junzi*] do not take leave of their authoritative conduct even for the space of a meal" (4.5). Even our most mundane experiences such as eating meals are infused with the magical power of *li*, that is, if one approaches *li* in the right way, in the spirit of *ren*.

The *junzi*, as the exemplary person, is one who through disciplined practice sets in motion a sympathetic vibration for others to follow. The path others will follow is the way of *yi*, appropriateness, rightness, or morality.[6] The way of *yi* will conflict with the mindless and self-directed acquisition of wealth and power. As the Master himself proclaims, "Exemplary persons (*junzi*) understand what is appropriate (*yi*); petty persons understand what is of personal advantage" (4.16).

Confucius seems to be aware that human seeking of personal advantage is often at the expense of someone else, and that the nature of our desires for self-fulfillment are self-perpetuating and self-accelerating. In the *Analects*, he writes, "To act with an eye to personal profit will incur a lot of resentment" (4.12) and "to eat coarse food, drink plain water, and pillow oneself on a bent arm—there is pleasure to be found in these things. But wealth and position gained through inappropriate means—these are to me like floating clouds" (7.16).[7] The simple life is extolled by Confucius as being a life of virtue because when we live "with an eye to personal profit," we are ruled by an addiction to pleasure, but remain unfulfilled.

The words of Confucius offer a good check against our current obsessions with self-satisfaction, self-esteem, and entitlement. Like many great religious leaders, the *junzi* will prefer death to the mere acquisition of wealth and power and to evil doing: "For the resolute scholar-apprentice and the authoritative person, while they would not compromise their authoritative conduct to save their lives, they might well give up their lives in order to achieve it" (15.9). Achieving *ren* is not rewarded by some better future incarnation, a mystical union with the Idea of the Good as we find in Plato's philosophy, or a place in heaven such as the promise of the Abrahamic traditions. The rewards promised by Confucius are deeper—our reward is one of connection in something greater than ourselves; our reward is one of fitting in, of finding one's place in the community and participating in traditions. This harmony of finding one's place is just not some ritualized form of hollow agreement that promotes the status quo. Rather, this harmony is a creative act that "requires the investment of oneself, one's judgment, and one's own sense of cultural importances" (Hall and Ames, 1998, 271).[8] Getting a life is to cultivate a creative participation within the community.

"The exemplary person (*junzi*) seeks harmony rather than agreement; the small person does the opposite" (13.23). The exemplary person must have the proprietorship of *yi*: "Having a sense of appropriate conduct (*yi*) as one's basic disposition, developing it in observing ritual propriety (*li*), expressing it with modesty, and consummating it in making good on one's word: this then is an exemplary person (*junzi*)" (15.18). Not only is the philosophy of Confucius central to understanding Chinese thought and culture, it offers different ways of thinking about life, death, and the communities from which we emerge and in which we invariably must participate. The message of Confucius is one of hope, a message without any appeals to and rewards from some eternal beyond. Confucius offers us a way in this world, a way that includes our fellow companions through the magical practice of *li*, a way where we become cultivated and live an authentic life full of meaning.

Biographical Sketch

Not much is known about the personal life of Confucius, or Master Kong, but we do know of his profound influence on Chinese civilization and its shaping of East and Southeast Asian cultures. Master Kong, or Kongzi, lived from 551-479 BCE and is well situated in what has been termed the Axial Age. It is astonishing to ponder how and why the end of the 6th Century BCE produced many of the world's seminal thinkers. These thinkers such as the Buddha, Zoroaster, Pythagoras, and Heracitus revolutionized their cultures and forever changed the world. Kongzi was one of these thinkers.

Like other seminal thinkers—Socrates, Buddha, Jesus—we are left with only accounts of Kongzi's life and the testimony of his teachings from his disciples. Shortly after he died, several disciples decided to inscribe the teachings of their master. This practice continued for a century and we are now left with the first ten books of the *Analects*. An additional ten books were added in the next century. Master Kong's philosophy developed during a savage time in Chinese history. Chinese history is marked by many wars and struggles, but the period known as the "Warring States Period" was especially devastating to the Chinese soul because it was a long and brutal civil war. The period lasted from 403-221 BCE, intensifying after the death of Confucius.

Kongzi was born in the state of Lu (today's Shangdong province) where he founded an academy. In this academy, he developed his philosophical vision through his teaching. His students would realize this vision, as did their master: through living a life based on practice. The more they practiced, the more they felt and experienced the teachings of the master as they made their own ways in living and dying. The emphasis on experiential learning and making one's own way in the context of one's accepted tradition was exemplified in the egalitarian and communal ethic of Confucius. He made no distinction whatsoever among the economic or social classes of his students; there was no standard tuition and fees—Kongzi would accept whatever his students could pay. What he did require from his students was the highest measure of commitment, seriousness, and enthusiasm for learning and living, which he considered synonymous with the good life.

At the Academy, students were delivered a liberal arts curriculum that prepared them for serving as good family members, friends, and citizens. Vocational training was seen as secondary and an outgrowth from developing and nurturing personal intimacy and integrity. The curriculum included physical education (archery and charioteering), math, writing, and music. But most notably was his emphasis on developing proficiency in observing *li*, or ritual propriety. Education for Confucius was all about developing character

—disclosing and opening the most opportune moment for the highest revelation of personhood to emerge.

Many of Kongzi's students found their way into political office. He himself is reported to have held some minor political office without much consequence. As a police commissioner, Confucius was humiliated in court (note that humiliation in the Chinese cultural context could be a matter of just not showing appropriate deference or being courteous) and later took to the road. In his fifties, he traveled from one state to the next to engage others, especially politicians, in conversation about virtue and the attainment of a good life. To the misfortune of the political leaders and the people of his day, his call for the good life landed on deaf ears, and as is the case with many revolutionary thinkers, he was sometimes threatened with death. Confucius returned to his home state of Lu, assumed a low level position as counselor, and continued his study. In 479 BCE, he died believing his life to be a failure.

When the Road is Smooth

The Master said, "Learn broadly of culture, discipline this learning through observing ritual propriety, and moreover, in so doing, remain on course without straying from it."

When the Road Gets Rocky

The Master said, "Zeng, my friend! My way is bound together by one continuous strand." Master Zeng replied, "Indeed."

When the Master had left, the disciples asked, "What was he referring to?" Master Zeng said, "The way of the Master is doing one's utmost and putting oneself in the other's place, nothing more."

When You Encounter a Dragon in the Middle of the Road

In Western mythologies, dragons are seen as fire breathing images of evil and need to be slain, but in the Chinese tradition the dragon has a much more positive image. The dragon swallows creatures whole, sheds its skin, and accumulates the features of every animal and becomes "the generative and transformative symbol of Chinese culture" (*Yuan Dao: Tracing Dao to Its Source*, Ballentine Books, New York, 1998, 43). When the *junzi* encounters the dragon in the middle of the road, he/she befriends the dragon because it is a symbol of change, accumulation, and integration. We, too, are part of this dragon, part of its journey, coursing its way through time and change. As Confucius reminds us, "It is the person who is able to broaden the way, not the way that broadens the person" (15.29).

The Crux: Confucius' Advice for Getting a Life

1. Do not do to others what you do not want them to do to you.
2. Always do one's utmost.
3. Eliminate profit and gain as motivations for personal achievement.
4. Remember that one's immediate personal success and achievement extends to everyone in one's community.
5. Perform even the most mundane tasks with mastery and in the spirit of human-heartedness and authenticity.
6. Abolish egocentricism and extend oneself into one's authentic tradition and community.
7. Realize that the success of those in one's community is also one's own.

In a Nutshell

The philosophy of life Confucius ascribes to abolishes egocentrism by returning to a sense of community and tradition. The result is a more satisfying life for the individual and a more harmonious and humane world.

The Wisdom of Confucius

On Self-Discipline
Yan Hui inquired about authoritative conduct (*ren*). The Master replied, "Through self-discipline and observing ritual propriety (*li*) one becomes authoritative in one's conduct. If for the space of a single day one were able to accomplish this, the whole

empire would defer to this authoritative model. Becoming authoritative in one's conduct is self-originating—how could it originate in others?" (12.1).

On Learning from Others

The Master said, "In strolling in the company of just two other persons, I am bound to find a teacher. Identifying their strengths, I follow them, and identifying their weaknesses, I reform myself accordingly" (7.22).

"When you meet persons of exceptional character think to stand shoulder to shoulder with them; meeting persons of little character, look inward and examine yourself" (4.17).

Important Dates

551 BCE	Confucius, Kongzi or Master Kong, born in the ancient state of Lu (Shangdong province).
479 BCE	Confucius dies thinking his life a failure.
479 BCE	Shortly after Kongzi's death, disciples begin writing down the "Sayings of Confucius."
372-289 BCE	Mengzi (Master Meng or Mencius) continues Confucius' legacy.
310-238 BCE	The legacy of Confucius continues with Xunzi or Master Xun.
960-1279 CE	Neo-Confucianism reaches its height during the Song Dynasty.
1966-1976	Cultural Revolution takes place in China. The *Pikong* ("Anti-Confucius Campaign") attempts a critique of Confucius by the entire literate Chinese population and ends up actually accomplishing the opposite.

References and Resources

Note: All parenthetical number (e.g. 4.12) citations are passages in the Analects.
Ames, R. T., & Rosemont H. 1998. *The Analects of Confucius: A Philosophical Translation.* New York: Ballentine Books. *By far the best translation of the Analects with an excellent introduction and notes.

Fingarette, H. 1972. *Confucius—The Secular as Sacred.* New York: Harper & Row.

Graham, A. C. 1989. *Disputers of the Tao: Philosophical Argument in Ancient China.* La Salle, Illinois: Open Court, 1989. *A scholarly but readable book on the complete ancient Chinese philosophical tradition.

Hall, D., & Ames, R. 1987. *Thinking Through Confucius.* Albany: State University of New York Press. *A landmark book that changed the course of interpretations of Confucius' thinking.

Hall, D. & Ames, R. 1998. *Thinking from the Han: Self, Truth, and Transcendence in Chinese and Western Culture.* Albany: State University of New York Press, 1998. *Picks up and develops threads of their earlier work, especially the one cited above.

Hall, D. & Ames, R. 1999. *The Democracy of the Dead: Dewey, Confucius, and the Hope for Democracy in China.* Chicago and Lasalle, Illinois: Open Court, 1999. *A radical, interesting, and readable study that applies the communitarian democratic philosophy of John Dewey and Confucius' philosophy to contemporary China.

Jones, D. 2000. "Teaching/Learning Through Confucius: Navigating our Way Through the Analects." In *Education About Asia* (Fall) 5(2).

Jones, D. & Culliney, J. 1988. "Confucian Order at the Edge of Chaos: The Science of Complexity and Ancient Wisdom." In *Zygon: Journal of Religion and Science*, Volume 33, Number 3, September 1988.

Lau, D. 1979. *Confucius: The Analects.* New York: Penguin Books. *A good translation of the *Analects*.

Rosemont, H. 1988. "Why Take Rights Seriously? A Confucian Critique." In *Human Rights and the World's Religions*, L. Rouner ed. Notre Dame, Indiana: University of Notre Dame Press.

Tu, Wei-ming 1985. *Confucian Thought: Selfhood as Creative Transformation.* Albany: State University of New York Press.

Notes

¹ Much of this chapter is borrowed from previously published work from "Teaching/Learning Through Confucius: Navigating our Way Through the Analects" (Education About Asia, 5, 2, Fall 2000 and "Finding Our Ways Through Chinese Classics: Reading the Analects of Confucius and the Zhuangzi" in *Extending the Boundaries: Approaches to World Literature*, Michael Tierce ed. Dubuque: Kendall/Hunt. 2000). In those works, as I do here, I acknowledge my debt to my teachers Graham Parkes and Roger Ames of the University of Hawaii at Manoa who provided an exemplary model for understanding the deeper Confucius. Throughout these works, I borrow heavily from their examples and present unabashedly a reading of Confucius' Analects deeply influenced and often similar to theirs.

² Herbert Fingarette, *Confucius—The Secular as Sacred*, 6. Fingarette has a good discussion on the sacred dimension of *li*. Although Fingarette has come under some attack by Chinese scholars for some of his interpretations, this book is still very useful and accessible.

³ For a more developed discussion of this aspect of Confucius's thinking see David Jones and John L. Culliney, "Confucian Order at the Edge of Chaos: The Science of Complexity and Ancient Wisdom," in *Zygon: Journal of Religion and Science*, September 1998, Volume 33 Number 3, 395-404.

⁴ I have intentionally left out the various degrees or levels of *ren* achievement such as *daren* (persons in high station), *shanren* (truly adept persons), *chengren* (consummate persons), *renzhe* or *renren* (authoritative persons), *shi* (scholar-apprentices), *junzi* (exemplary persons), and *shen* or *shengren* (sages) for purposes of simplification. See Roger T. Ames and Henry Rosemont Jr., *The Analects of Confucius: A Philosophical Translation*, 60 for further discussion of the last three categories of *ren* listed above.

⁵ See Roger T. Ames and Henry Rosemont Jr., *The Analects of Confucius: A Philosophical Translation*, 48 for a discussion on two possible etymologies of ren.

⁶ *Yi* is often considered a central term for the ethical dimension of Confucius's thought in the following ways: (1)When applied to a particular act, *yi* will usually mean "right" as in "that was the right action to take" or "that was the right thing to do." (2) In discussions about kinds of actions, *yi* means duty, the act that one ought to perform in a given particular situation.

(3) When *yi* is applied to agents who perform a right act, *yi* means righteous, dutiful, or moral person. Further, given the Confucius's relational sense of self, *yi* is usually used in reference to acts while *ren* is used to characterize persons. These distinctions of *yi*, however, fall under the governance of yi as appropriateness or fittingness and harmony (he)—one ought to find his or her proper place within a broader context. *Li* always provides this wider context. See Roger T. Ames and Henry Rosemont Jr., *The Analects of Confucius: A Philosophical Translation*, 53, for demarcating *yi* from a Western ethical understanding.

[7] See also 14.1, 1.15, and 4.9.

[8] See also 1.12, 2.14, and 15.22.

NOTES

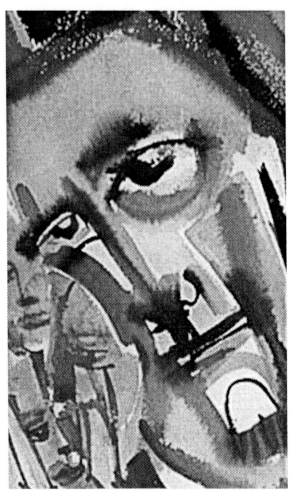

Courtesy of Paulist Press

RICHARD OF ST. VICTOR

(1123?-1173)

By Wade Carpenter

Little is known about the life of Richard of St. Victor, other than that he was born in Scotland, and joined the Canons Regular of St. Victor of Paris (a monastery) sometime in the 1150s, becoming prior (2nd-ranking office) of their abbey in 1162. Just down the street from the future Sorbonne, the abbey was the intellectual and spiritual center of Europe. Richard of St. Victor's biographical anonymity suits him. He was a humble figure surrounded by giants such as Bernard of Clairvaux, William of St. Thierry, Peter Abelard, and his own predecessor, Hugh of St. Victor. His thought, on the other hand, is well-known among monastics, but heretofore neglected by just about everyone else. This is unfortunate, because Richard was the bridge between the contemplative spirituality of monastic education and a new intellectualism, which would ultimately lead to the development of universities.

Richard's The Twelve Patriarchs, *also referred to as* Benjamin Minor, *uses the Biblical family of Jacob allegorically to provide a 13-step curriculum taking the soul from fearful penitence to the heights of contemplative spirituality. Combined with other contemporary innovations (see Illich, 1990, 1993), Richard's curriculum ultimately led to the synthesis of faith and reason accomplished by St. Thomas Aquinas, and from there, Christian Humanism, the Scientific Revolution, and finally, the modern era itself.*

Although Richard's writings are explicitly religious, his allegories hold much value for the nonreligious as well. Richard of St. Victor is the quiet voice of intelligent spirituality and systematic personal development, a voice that helped heal the growing rift between the "spirituals" and the "intellectuals" of his time. His curriculum bears startling similarities to the 12 Steps of Alcoholics Anonymous, and can provide a useful framework for living in an age of fluctuating values, media overload, and growing materialism.

> The Holy Spirit in no way makes fruitful a mind that, when advised by reason, does not moderate its appetite for vain praise.

Reason, Resulting in Truth

The Twelve Patriarchs is an outgrowth of a peculiar way of reading, *lectio divina*, which is quite foreign to those of us brought up to think of the printed word as informational, something to be gotten through quickly, perhaps to be analyzed later. *Lectio* is a SLOWWWW reading of texts of lasting or sacred value, in which every line is prized, and the author considered a "partner in truth" rather than a target for critique. In the monastery, slow devotional reading of a text would be followed by intellectually strenuous meditation, followed by quiet contemplation, in which the mind is quieted in order to hear God. The great Jewish philosopher Moses Maimonides set out a similar approach to devotions, in which roughly a third of the time is for acquisition of information, a third for analysis, and a third for reflection (Ulich, 1954, 651-662; see also Illich, 1993; Pennington, 1998; http://www. lectiodivina.org/).

Lectio is supposed to result in a wordless experience of God Himself, but sometimes the process elicits thoughts filled with self-revelation, heavily laced with analogy, metaphor, and simile. Richard is a master allegorist and *The Twelve Patriarchs* is an allegory based upon the characters and events of Genesis 29-50.

In case you are unfamiliar with the story, there is a man, Jacob, who falls in love with the younger daughter, Rachel, of a man named Laban. Jacob asks Laban if he can marry Rachel and Laban says, "Okay, but you have to work for me for seven years first." So, Jacob works for Laban for seven years. When the day of the marriage finally arrives, Laban pulls a switch and offers his older daughter Leah as a bride to Jacob rather than Rachel. Understandably, Jacob gets angry and demands the hand of Rachel. Laban tells Jacob (albeit a little belatedly) that it is improper for the younger daughter in a family to be married before the elder. So, he must marry Leah first, and then work another seven years for the hand of Rachel. Jacob consents to this arrangement and, in another seven years, finally marries Rachel.

Because of her status as an emotional outcast, Richard sees Jacob's unloved first wife Leah as a trope for affection. Rachel, beautiful and clear sighted, represents reason. Jacob is associated with intelligence. The offspring of Jacob correlate to the steps of Richard's curriculum. The steps must be taken in order and are as follows:
1. fear,
2. the contrition that follows fear,
3. the hope given upon repentance,
4. the love which arises in response,
5. the prudence with which we look ahead for dangers,
6. the disciplined will which arises from prudence,
7. temperance in prosperity,
8. patience in hardship,
9. the radiance that comes from God's presence,
10. the zeal with which we often respond to God's presence,
11. the shame that follows when we allow our zeal to affect our common sense and compassion,
12. the discretion that we learn as a result of shame, and finally,
13. the grace of direct experience of the Divine.
The grace of God (No. 13) is the culmination of the sequence, the full realization of human potential.

Fear and Contrition: The Beginning of Wisdom

Popular psychology often sees fear as an evil to avoid. Richard is smarter than that. He knows its value. Richard uses the birth of Jacob's first son by Leah to illustrate the role of fear in the soul's development:
> When the Lord saw that Leah was unloved, he opened her womb; but Rachel was barren. Leah conceived and bore a son, and she named him Reuben, for she said 'Because the LORD has looked on

my affliction; surely now my husband will love me.' (Genesis 29: 31, 32)

Richard translates "Reuben" as "Son of Vision," leading to a point most self-help writers miss entirely, that fear can be a strong, effective motivator.

> It is written: 'The fear of the Lord is the beginning of wisdom' (Ps 111:10). Therefore this offspring is the first of the virtues. Without it you are not able to have others. . . . At his birth his mother rightly exclaims 'God has seen my abasement' because from that time she should begin to see and to be seen; to know God and to be known by God; to see God through the intuition of dread; to be seen by God through the regard of kindness (Richard of St. Victor, 1979, VIII, 60).

Leah's "son of vision" was the outcome of the fear of being unloved, and the vision of relief from that fear. Every human being deals with fear of something. Death is, of course, the biggie. As the poster says, "That which does not kill me. . . postpones the inevitable." To be unprepared for life is unfortunate; to be unprepared for death is just dumb. But the fear that Richard discusses is only partly negative. It is not just the sort of terror of an eighteen wheeler skidding into our lane, but a sense of awe accompanying our first vague impressions of God.

This mixture of fear and awe is akin to seeing the Grand Canyon for the first time. While the sight of the canyon is beautiful, it is also a little frightening. The Canyon has steep cliffs, and, if you slipped, you might fall to your death.

Fear is Richard's first step. This fear is the realization that sooner or later one will die, and if there really is a God and He doesn't like being ignored, one may be in for a world of hurt. But like the Grand Canyon, Richard's God is also breathtaking and compellingly attractive. If we choose, both the awe of the canyon and the fear of God resolve into a consuming desire to see more and go deeper.

After fear, the next step is sorrow or contrition, an essential part of addressing fear. Richard identifies contrition with Leah's second son, Simeon, whose name refers to the Lord "having heard" (*shm'a*) her sorrow. While it would be cruel to deny praise and support to those whom life has savaged, it is foolish to lavish it on the smug. For someone who thinks he has all the answers, there may be little incentive for learning. Sorrow, contrition, and humility open us up to learning.

Here the traditional calendars of the major faiths are helpful, designating and limiting the periods of fasting and penance, providing time for feasts and celebrations, and insisting on a weekly day of rest. With such guidance, and that of an experienced and sensitive shepherd, contrition is not an unwholesome neurosis. Like childbirth, it is a pain that produces new life. Undertaken honestly and with level-headed courage, it can lead to exultation.

Hope and Love

The allegorical connections between fear and contrition and hope and love are made through Leah's next two children, Levi and Judah. Richard associates Levi with "hope" through the redemptive role of Levi's priestly descendants. The patronymic, in fact, comes from a root meaning "attached" or "added." Richard comments:

> The divine word does not call this son 'given' but 'added' lest anyone presume to have hope of forgiveness before fear and grief worthy of repentance. For whoever compliments himself with impunity after committing crimes without satisfaction is not so much raised up by hope as he is thrown down by presumption (X, 62).

Unfortunately, the "cheap grace" pushed by some televangelists seems founded upon just such a presumption. Christ pointed out that simply having a troubled conscience without giving satisfaction for the wrongs one has done is insufficient:

> If thou bring thy gift to the altar and there rememberest that thy brother hath ought against thee: Leave there thy gift before the altar, and go thy way; first be reconciled to thy brother, and then come and offer thy gift (Matthew 5:23-24).

When you wrong someone, you must acknowledge, repent, and reconcile the deed; otherwise, you remain complacent and in denial.

Jacob and Leah's fourth child's name, Judah, is like the "adoration" we associate with someone who has just fallen in love. The feeling can be as joyous as Marius's pinings after Cosette in *Les Miserables*, but is more spiritual. In *Fiddler on the Roof*, the character of Tevye depicts this love wistfully

> If I were rich I'd have the time that I lack to sit in the synagogue and pray
> And maybe have a seat by the eastern wall
> And I'd discuss the holy books with the learned men seven hours

every day
And that would be the sweetest thing of all ....

This passion for God and His teachings is a gift, but not one to be confused with gushing infatuation. Infatuation is just something that gets 16-year-olds in trouble. Adoration, on the other hand, is a learned behavior, and there are many ways to acquire it. In Philippians 4:8 St. Paul suggests beginning with a simple therapeutic shift of attention on what is right with the world.

> Finally, brethren, whatsoever things are true, whatsoever things are honest, whatsoever things are just, whatsoever things are pure, whatsoever things are lovely, whatsoever things are of good report: If there be any virtue, and if there be any praise, think on these things.

Adoration does not require any advanced degree. In fact, the affection that starts the process arises out of purely natural needs. But Richard goes further. If adoration remains static, without intellectual or spiritual components, we remain immature. To grow, you need to develop both mind and soul.

Prudence and an Educated Will

Leah's "blind affection" has proven fertile, and after the birth of Judah (adoration), she feels satisfied. However, Richard explains that an ordered affection for God such as that symbolized by Judah motivates us to want to know more about God. At this point the intellect gets involved. Rachel is resentful toward her rival and longs for children, but cannot seem to get pregnant.

So Rachel gives Jacob her handmaiden Bilhah (whom Richard associates with "imagination"), who thereupon produces two sons, Dan and Naphtali. Because persons with good imaginations also need good judgment, Richard translates "Dan" as "prudence." Naphtali, on the other hand, means "wrestling." Just as Jacob was victorious in his wrestling with God, so Naphtali is a victorious wrestler of the will. An educated will involves understanding, action, and habit. To be both determined and intelligent involves social as well as personal virtues. Personal character alone is not sufficient for getting a good life. Without the balance of the intellect, personal virtue tends toward stuffiness or moralism. Without character, intellect can be used for evil purposes.

Temperance and Patience

Prudence and willpower help us control our appetites, and produce temperance in plenty and patience in suffering. Richard lays the scriptural basis for this by recounting how, envious of Rachel's success as an adoptive mother; Leah gives Jacob her servant Zelpha, whom Richard allegorizes as sensation. She bears two sons, and poor old Leah declares that she is finally "happy" with little Gad, and "blessed" with Asher.

Richard evokes the axiom "Moderation in all things" (in all things except family size apparently) and identifies happiness with temperance in prosperity. He gets more Semitic, though, with Asher who represents patience in suffering. The idea of patient suffering is the antithesis of instant gratification so prevalent in popular culture. To associate moderation with happiness and endurance with blessedness is way out of line with our fast food, "give it to me now" mindset. Richard implies that humble moderation may beget a more enduring happiness, a contentedness that cannot only endure suffering, but transcend it.

Radiance and Zeal

It is hardly surprising that temperance and patience would have salutary effects on one's personality. They help foster a "sweetness" of disposition. The child next born to Leah is Isaachar, which in Hebrew means "reward." Richard emphasizes that Isaachar's reward will be to settle in a "sweet land" half-within, half-outside the promised land. But he will quickly become complacent, and ultimately, will serve the others. Unfortunately, our modern usage of the word "sweet" evokes an image of naiveté, sentimentalism, and effeminacy inconsistent with what Richard intended. A closer approximation would be "radiance." Learners at Isaachar's stage, according to Richard, are privy to "a foretaste of glory divine."

When enjoyed rightly, Richard notes, radiance strengthens the soul and inclines it toward humble things. Not properly ordered, it becomes tacky. The country that gave the world paintings of Elvis on velvet and commercials for balding, impotence, breast enlargements, and incontinence at suppertime would benefit from Richard's insight into the souls of the silly. Isaachar ends up in a dumb, happy servitude, but he finds that after awhile, he craves the blessings that lie beyond bliss.

> Isaachar has almost, but not completely, abandoned that land of the dying, and almost but not completely grasped the land of the living.

A yearning for heaven is characteristic of the soul at the radiance stage. But without a "real world" balance, you remain radiant, but become so self-satisfied that you fail to make a significant contribution. So, the next child, Zebulon, whose name Richard translates as "dwelling place of fortitude" is protective and corrective.

> [He] grows strong in the hatred of all vices to such an extent that now it is not enough for him not to consent to receive any vices in himself unless he is also zealous to pursue them manfully in others and to strike them with strong chastisement.

The problem with Zebulons is that they can often become zealots who love humanity but hate humans. Who hasn't run afoul of the absurd phrase from the sixties, "If you're not part of the solution, you're part of the problem?" Taken to its extreme, zeal can become the rationale of the terrorist, who fails to see any other perspective than his/her own. At this stage of spiritual development, self-effacing humor is usually better than self-righteous severity.

Shame and Discretion

To paraphrase the bumper sticker, shame happens, and when it happens we usually try to minimize it with false bravado or crass attempts at comedy. But shame is often needed; a shameless society is dangerous. The Holocaust, sexual shenanigans among politicians, and the nonchalant acceptance of heinous crimes demonstrate the horrors of shamelessness. But *imposing* shame on others is seldom moral. Nonetheless, shame can be useful, especially if you refuse to descend into the gloomy claustrophobia of moralism. In general, catharsis is much healthier than denial.

Leah's last child is a girl, Dinah, who grows up lovely and gentle. One day, she is noticed by the mayor's son, Shechem, who is instantly smitten. Tragically, the boy is not accustomed to hearing the word "no," and rapes her. Dinah is dishonored. Her brothers, who should have been protecting her, are shamed by their negligence. Moderate shame is a good thing; obsessive shame is not. The brothers obsess.

As it turns out, Shechem falls in love with Dinah and is willing to do right by her, which seems to be agreeable to her and her father. Her brothers, however, cunningly add a rather demanding codicil to the wedding contract: Shechem and all his retainers must undergo circumcision. Shechem's love for Dinah is so ardent that he agrees.

Unfortunately, on the third day after the circumcision, when postoperative soreness was at its worst, Levi and Simeon murder Shechem and all his men, and the rest of the brothers join in pillaging their property, shaming everyone. As previously noted, Simeon symbolizes contrition and Levi hope. Contrition gone wrong becomes depression, despair, and rage, in other words, insanity. And if one's hope rests only in human values, retributive justice becomes just about necessary if one is to believe in justice at all.

Nevertheless, even at this sad stage, God's people are redeemable. Jacob's favored wife, Rachel (whom Richard associates with "reason"), finally bears a son, Joseph. Richard associates Joseph with "discretion." Joseph eventually becomes a master of wise counsel in Egypt. Richard notes that Joseph becomes successful only after an episode of terrible shame, a "Dark Night of the Soul." Although Joseph starts out pretty uppity, after much hardship, he far exceeds his brothers in all the virtues.

Contemplation and Divine Grace

Richard associates Jacob's last child, Benjamin, with contemplation, based on a passage from the Psalms (Psalm 67: 28). Benjamin marks a departure from the rational, since Rachel ("reason") dies giving birth to him. Contemplation is more than meditation; it is something beyond human reason. According to Richard, contemplation is an attentive, *sometimes* ecstatic, experience of God. Reason will take us to the point of grace, but no further. Through contemplation, you enter the realm of the spiritual. This highest stage of spiritual growth comes only after many years of fear, contrition, hope, love, prudence, spiritual understanding, temperance, patience, radiance, zeal, shame, and discretion within a community of faith. Richard is prudent regarding the dangers of privileged knowledge and interaction with the divine. While many religious leaders may tend towards excess, Richard advo-

cates reverence and common sense. By encountering the world through a well
-developed balance of sensory perceptions, intellect, and spirit, you begin to
fulfill your potential as a human being.

When the Road is Smooth

When the road is smooth, be thankful. Gratitude combines reason
with affection, thus making a rich relationship with God possible. But keep
your good fortune in perspective. Use temperance in times of plenty.

When the Road Gets Rocky

If the road is rocky as the result of your overconfidence, then a
healthy dose of fear is what you need. The road can always get rockier, and
unless you change your attitude, things will probably get worse. As Reuben
gave way to the second son, Simeon, so should fear help point you in the right
direction.

However, if your problems are not your fault, but the result of someone else's misdeeds, remember when Rachel's father tricked Jacob into seven
extra years' labor if he wanted to wed the more attractive daughter. Like
Jacob, you would be wise to keep your focus on that which you really love.
Richard wrote, "The days seemed few to him because of the greatness of
love."

When You Encounter a Dragon in the Middle of the Road

Other generations would refer to Richard's dragon by various names,
including "Leviathan," "The Cloud of Unknowing," and "The Dark Night of
the Soul." Jacob's family expends great effort and energy to overcome the
dragon—Rachel's barrenness—but nothing works. Although each "offspring"
makes a contribution to the family, Rachel's faithfulness is what really counts.
Only by joyfully overcoming obstacles through faith can you come to know
God.

The Crux: Richard St. Victor's Advice for Getting a Life

Richard describes thirteen stages of spiritual development, each stage more sophisticated, fulfilling, and virtuous than the previous one. However, every stage holds the possibility for mistakes and abuse. For example, ministers who possess religious zeal may have successfully navigated through fear, contrition, hope, love, prudence, discipline, temperance in prosperity, patience in hardship, and radiance. But, if they think that they know all the answers and speak against believers of other faiths, then they are perverting their power and misdirecting their energy.

To live up to your potential, you must maintain a sense of humility, develop wholesome habits, and work tirelessly to develop your hands, head, heart, and soul. As soon as you get lazy and comfortable in your spiritual growth, you lose it.

In a Nutshell

The rocky road is inevitable; it is nothing to fear. The dragon might not be an enemy after all. In fact, fear of the dragon is the first step towards a better life.

The Wisdom of Richard St. Victor

On Intellect and Faith
When we consider how much the philosophers of this world have laboured, we should be ashamed to be inferior to them....We should seek always to comprehend by reason what we hold by faith.

On Negativity
There are many who blame themselves for a perverse work or a depraved will. There are few who judge themselves for a disordered thought.

On Knowing Yourself
If you are not able to know yourself, how do you have the boldness to grasp at those things which are above you?

On Contemplation

[Contemplation is] seeing truth in purity and simplicity.

On Losing Your Mind

To be led above ourselves...with so much alienation of soul that for a while our mind might know nothing of itself while it is astounded as it is suspended in the viewing of such cherubim (1979, 272).

Important Dates

1128	Hugh of St. Victor begins his *Didascalicon*, a manual on teaching and learning, Victorine-style.
1141	Abelard's rationalist philosophy condemned by Bernard of Clairvaux
1153	Richard begins *The Twelve Patriarchs*
1180	Oxford University established
1215	In England, King John signs the Magna Carta
1253	Robert de Sorbon founds the University of Paris.
1266	St. Thomas Aquinas begins the *Summa Theologica*

References and Resources

Carpenter, W. A. 2000. *Behind Every Silver Lining: The Other Side of Student Centeredness*. Educational Horizons, 78 (4): 205-210.

Carpenter, W. A. 1999. "Magnanimity, Virtue Ethics, and Teacher Education." in *Religion and Education*, 26 (1): 58-64.

Hicks, D. V. 1999. *Norms and Nobility: A Treatise on Education*. New York: University Press of America.

Illich, I. 1990. *In the Vineyard of the Text*. NPQ, 7 (4): 56-58.

Illich, I. 1993. *In the Vineyard of the Text*. Chicago: University of Chicago Press.

John of the Cross, St. 1574/1959. *The Dark Night of the Soul* (E. Allison Peers, Trans). (3d ed). New York: Image.

Lickona, T. 1991. *Educating for Character: How Our Schools Can Teach Respect and Responsibility*. New York: Basic.

Lafort, R. 1912. *The Catholic Encyclopedia, Volume XIII* (1912). New York: Robert Appleton Company. Online Edition available: http://www.newadvent.org/cathen/13045c.htm

Pennington, M. B. 1998. *Lectio Divina*. New York: Crossroad.

Richard of St. Victor. 1979. *The Twelve Patriarchs, The Mystical Ark, Book Three of the Trinity* (Grover A. Zinn, Trans.). The Classics of Western Spirituality. Mahwah, NJ: Paulist Press.

Sertillanges, A. G. 1987. *The Intellectual Life—Its Spirits, Conditions, Methods.* Washington, D.C.: The Catholic University of America Press.

Ulich, R. 1954. *Three Thousand Years of Educational Wisdom.* Cambridge: Harvard University Press.

NOTES

THE EDITORS

Lawrence Baines is a professor of education at The University of Toledo. He writes on creative approaches to teaching and living. Baines lives in Ohio with his wife and son.

Dan McBrayer has been a college professor, husband, father and mentor for more than thirty years. Having served as an academic dean, a department head, and in an endowed chair in psychology, Dan has received multiple awards for teaching excellence. He has made hundreds of presentations around the country, and for the last twenty-four years has taught at Berry College in Rome, GA.

The editors wish to express their gratitude to Donna Davin, Alisa Ray, Mariella Griffiths, Sharon McBrayer, Juanita Cordle, Merrill Davies, Kathy Gann, Coleen Baines, and Chris Walker for their immense help with this book.

THE CONTRIBUTORS

Each of the fifteen chapters was written by a different contributor/expert. The contributors of each chapter are listed in the Table of Contents. Without them, this book would not be in your hands at this moment. We are very grateful to them for their contributions and enthusiasm in this project.

THE SERIES

This book is the first in the series *How To Get A Life*. We hope you enjoyed it and found some of the information helpful and inspirational. The second book will be available in fall 2003. While the focus of this volume is on humanitarians and spiritual leaders, the focus of the second volume will be on thinkers and writers. Subsequent volumes, highlighting the experiences, habits, and beliefs of eminent men and women who "made a mark," may be possible. We will continue to work to develop material that is interesting, useful, and life-affirming. Thank you and best wishes.

Printed in the United States
1275200004B/67-123